CW00486759

Marco Paul's Voyages

Vermont

Jacob Abbott

Alpha Editions

This edition published in 2022

ISBN : 9789356786745

Design and Setting By
Alpha Editions
www.alphaedis.com
Email - info@alphaedis.com

As per information held with us this book is in Public Domain.
This book is a reproduction of an important historical work. Alpha Editions uses the
best technology to reproduce historical work in the same manner it was first
published to preserve its original nature. Any marks or number seen are left
intentionally to preserve its true form.

Contents

PREFACE.

The design of the series of volumes, entitled MARCO PAUL'S ADVENTURES IN THE PURSUIT OF KNOWLEDGE, is not merely to entertain the reader with a narrative of juvenile adventures, but also to communicate, in connection with them, as extensive and varied information as possible, in respect to the geography, the scenery, the customs and the institutions of this country, as they present themselves to the observation of the little traveler, who makes his excursions under the guidance of an intelligent and well-informed companion, qualified to assist him in the acquisition of knowledge and in the formation of character. The author has endeavored to enliven his narrative, and to infuse into it elements of a salutary moral influence, by means of personal incidents befalling the actors in the story. These incidents are, of course, imaginary--but the reader may rely upon the strict and exact truth and fidelity of all the descriptions of places, institutions and scenes, which are brought before his mind in the progress of the narrative. Thus, though the author hopes that the readers who may honor these volumes with their perusal, will be amused and interested by them, his design throughout will be to instruct rather than to entertain.

CHAPTER I.

JOURNEYING.

When Mr. Baron, Marco's father, put Marco under his cousin Forester's care, it was his intention that he should spend a considerable part of his time in traveling, and in out-of-door exercises, such as might tend to re-establish his health and strengthen his constitution. He did not, however, intend to have him give up the study of books altogether. Accordingly, at one time, for nearly three months, Marco remained at Forester's home, among the Green Mountains of Vermont, where he studied several hours every day.

It was in the early part of the autumn, that he and Forester went to Vermont. They traveled in the stage-coach. Vermont lies upon one side of the Connecticut river, and New Hampshire upon the other side. The Green Mountains extend up and down, through the middle of Vermont, from north to south, and beyond these mountains, on the western side of the state, is lake Champlain, which extends from north to south also, and forms the western boundary. Thus, the Green Mountains divide the state into two great portions, one descending to the eastward, toward Connecticut river, and the other to the westward, toward lake Champlain. There are, therefore, two great ways of access to Vermont from the states south of it; one up the Connecticut river on the eastern side, and the other along the shores of lake George and lake Champlain on the western side. There are roads across the Green Mountains also, leading from the eastern portion of the state to the western. All this can be seen by looking upon any map of Vermont.

Marco and Forester went up by the Connecticut river. The road lay along upon the bank of the river, and the scenery was very pleasant. They traveled in the stage-coach; for there were very few railroads in those days.

The country was cultivated and fertile, and the prospect from the windows of the coach was very fine. Sometimes wide meadows and intervales extended along the river,--and at other places, high hills, covered with trees, advanced close to the stream. They could see, too, the farms, and villages, and green hills, across the river, on the New Hampshire side.

On the second day of their journey, they turned off from the river by a road which led into the interior of the country; for the village where Forester's father resided was back among the mountains. They had new companions in the coach too, on this second day, as well as a new route; for the company which had been in the coach the day before were to separate in the morning, to go off in different directions. Several stage-coaches drove up to the door of the tavern in the morning, just after breakfast, with the names of the places where they were going to, upon their sides. One was marked, "Haverhill and Lancaster;" another, "Middlebury;" and a third, "Concord and Boston;" and there was one odd-looking vehicle, a sort of carryall, open in front, and drawn by two horses, which had no name upon it, and so Marco could not tell where it was going. As these several coaches and carriages drove up to the door, the hostlers and drivers put on the baggage and bound it down with great straps, and then handed in the passengers;--and thus the coaches, one after another, drove away. The whole movement formed a very busy scene, and Marco, standing upon the piazza in front of the tavern, enjoyed it very much.

There was a very large elm-tree before the door, with steps to climb up, and seats among the branches. Marco went up there and sat some time, looking down upon the coaches as they wheeled round the tree, in coming up to the door. Then he went down to the piazza again.

THE GREAT ELM.

The Great Elm

There was a neatly-dressed young woman, with a little flower-pot in her hand, standing near him, waiting for her turn. There was a small orange-tree in her flower-pot. It was about six inches high. The sight of this orange-tree interested Marco very much, for it reminded him of home. He had often seen orange-trees growing in the parlors and green-houses in New York.

"What a pretty little orange-tree!" said Marco. "Where did you get it?"

"How did you know it was an orange-tree?" said the girl.

"O, I know an orange-tree well enough," replied Marco. "I have seen them many a time."

"Where?" asked, the girl.

"In New York," said Marco. "Did your orange-tree come from New York?"

"No," said the girl. "I planted an orange-seed, and it grew from that. I've got a lemon-tree, too," she added, "but it is a great deal larger. The lemon-tree grows faster than the orange. My lemon-tree is so large that I couldn't bring it home very well, so I left it in the mill."

"In the mill?" said Marco. "Are you a miller?"

The girl laughed. She was a very good-humored girl, and did not appear to be displeased, though it certainly was not quite proper for Marco to speak in that manner to a stranger. She did not, however, reply to his question, but said, after a pause,

"Do you know where the Montpelier stage is?"

The proper English meaning of the word *stage* is a *portion of the road*, traveled between one resting-place and another. But in the United States it is used to mean the carriage,--being a sort of contraction for *stage-coach*.

"No," said Marco, "*we* are going in that stage."

"I wish it would come along," said the girl, "for I'm tired of watching my trunk."

"Where is your trunk?" said Marco.

So the girl pointed out her trunk. It was upon the platform of the piazza, near those belonging to Forester and Marco. The girl showed Marco her name, which was Mary Williams, written on a card upon the end of it.

"I'll watch your trunk," said Marco, "and you can go in and sit down until the stage comes."

Mary thanked him and went in. She was not, however, quite sure that her baggage was safe, intrusted thus to the charge of a strange boy, and so she took a seat near the window, where she could keep an eye upon it. There was a blue chest near these trunks, which looked like a sailor's chest, and Marco, being tired of standing, sat down upon this chest. He had, however, scarcely taken his seat, when he saw a coach with four horses, coming round a corner. It was driven by a small boy not larger than Marco. It wheeled up toward the door, and came to a stand. Some men then put on the sailor's chest and the trunks. Mary Williams came out and got into the coach. She sat on the back seat. Forester and Marco got in, and took their places on the middle seat. A young man, dressed like a sailor, took the front seat, at one corner of the coach. These were all the passengers that were to get in here. When every thing was ready, they drove away.

The stage stopped, however, in a few minutes at the door of a handsome house in the town, and took a gentleman and lady in. These new passengers took places on the back seat, with Mary Williams.

This company rode in perfect silence for some time. Forester took out a book and began to read. The gentleman on the back seat went to sleep. Mary Williams and Marco looked out at the windows, watching the changing scenery. The sailor rode in silence; moving his lips now and then, as if he were talking to himself, but taking no notice of any of the company. The coach stopped at the villages which they passed through, to exchange the mail, and sometimes to take in new passengers. In the course of these changes Marco got his place shifted to the forward seat by the side of the sailor, and he gradually got into conversation with him. Marco introduced the conversation, by asking the sailor if he knew how far it was to Montpelier.

"No," said the sailor, "I don't keep any reckoning, but I wish we were there."

"Why?" asked Marco.

"O, I expect the old cart will capsize somewhere among these mountains, and break our necks for us."

Marco had observed, all the morning, that when the coach canted to one side or the other, on account of the unevenness of the road, the sailor always started and looked anxious, as if afraid it was going to be upset. He wondered that a man who had been apparently accustomed to the terrible dangers of the seas, should be alarmed at the gentle oscillations of a stage-coach.

"Are you afraid that we shall upset?" asked Marco.

"Yes," said the sailor, "over some of these precipices and mountains; and then there'll be an end of us."

The sailor said this in an easy and careless manner, as if, after all, he was not much concerned about the danger. Still, Marco was surprised that he should fear it at all. He was not aware how much the fears which people feel, are occasioned by the mere novelty of the danger which they incur. A stage-driver, who is calm and composed on his box, in a dark night, and upon dangerous roads, will be alarmed by the careening of a ship under a gentle breeze at sea,--while the sailor who laughs at a gale of wind on the ocean, is afraid to ride in a carriage on land.

"An't you a sailor?" asked Marco.

"Yes," replied his companion.

"I shouldn't think that a man that had been used to the sea, would be afraid of upsetting in a coach."

"I'm not a *man*" said the sailor.

"What are you?" said Marco.

"I'm a boy. I'm only nineteen years old; though I'm going to be rated seaman next voyage."

"Have you just got back from a voyage?" asked Marco.

"Yes," said the sailor. "I've been round the Horn in a whaler, from old Nantuck. And now I'm going home to see my mother."

"How long since you've seen her?" asked Marco.

"O, it's four years since I ran away."

Here the sailor began to speak in rather a lower tone than he had done before, so that Marco only could hear. This was not difficult, as the other passengers were at this time engaged in conversation.

"I ran away," continued the sailor, "and went to sea about four years ago."

"What made you run away?" asked Marco.

"O, I didn't want to stay at home and be abused. My father used to abuse me; but my mother took my part, and now I want to go and see her."

"And to see your father too," said Marco.

"No," said the sailor. "I don't care for him. I hope he's gone off somewhere. But I want to see my mother. I have got a shawl for her in my chest."

Marco was shocked to hear a young man speak in such a manner of his father. Still there was something in the frankness and openness of the sailor's manner, which pleased him very much. He liked to hear his odd and sailor-like language too, and he accordingly entered into a long conversation with him. The sailor gave him an account of his adventures on the voyage; how he was drawn off from the ship one day, several miles, by a whale which they had harpooned;--how they caught a shark, and hauled him in on deck by means of a pulley at the end of the yard-arm;--and how, on the voyage home, the ship was driven before an awful gale of wind for five days, under bare poles, with terrific seas roaring after them all the way. These descriptions took a strong hold of Marco's imagination. His eye brightened up, and he became restless on his seat, and thought that he would give the world for a chance to stand up in the bow of a boat, and put a harpoon into the neck of a whale.

In the mean time, the day wore away, and the road led into a more and more mountainous country. The hills were longer and steeper, and the tracts of forest more frequent and solitary. The number of passengers increased too, until the coach was pretty heavily loaded; and sometimes all but the female passengers would get out and walk up the hills. On these occasions Forester and Marco would generally walk together, talking about the incidents of their journey, or the occupations and amusements which they expected to engage in when they arrived at Forester's home. About the middle of the afternoon the coach stopped at the foot of a long winding ascent, steep and stony, and several of the passengers got out. Forester, however, remained in, as he was tired of walking, and so Marco and the sailor walked together. The sailor, finding how much Marco was interested in his stories, liked his company, and at length he asked Marco where he was going. Marco told him.

"Ah, if you were only going on a voyage with me," said the sailor, "that would make a man of you. I wouldn't go and be shut up with that old prig, poring over books forever."

Marco was displeased to hear the sailor call his cousin an old prig, and he felt some compunctions of conscience about forming and continuing an intimacy with such a person. Still he was so much interested in hearing him talk, that he continued to walk with him up the hill. Finally, the sailor fairly proposed to him to run away and go to sea with him.

"O no," said Marco, "I wouldn't do such a thing for the world. Besides," said he, "they would be after us, and carry me back."

"No," said the sailor; "we would cut across the country, traveling in the night and laying to by day, till we got to another stage route, and then make a straight wake, till we got to New Bedford, and there we could get a good voyage. Come," said he, "let's go to-night. I'll turn right about. I don't care a great deal about seeing my mother."

Though Marco was a very bold and adventurous sort of a boy, still he was not quite prepared for such a proposal as this. In the course of the conversation the sailor used improper and violent language too, which Marco did not like to hear; and, in fact, Marco began to be a little afraid of his new acquaintance. He determined, as soon as he got back to the coach to keep near Forester all the time, so as not to be left alone again with the sailor. He tried to hasten on, so as to overtake the coach, but the sailor told him not to walk so fast; and, being unwilling to offend him, he was obliged to go slowly, and keep with him; and thus protracted the conversation.

T :   H ! L L,

The Hill.

About half-way up the hill there was a small tavern, and the sailor wanted Marco to go in with him and get a drink. Marco thought that he meant a drink of water, but it was really a drink of spirits which was intended. Marco, however, refused to go, saying that he was not thirsty; and so they went on up the hill. At the top of the hill, the stage-coach stopped for the pedestrians to come up. There was also another passenger there to get in,--a woman, who came out from a farm-house near by. The driver asked the sailor if he was not willing to ride outside, in order to make room for the new passenger. But he would not. He was afraid. He said he would not ride five miles outside for a month's wages. Marco laughed at the sailor's fears, and he immediately asked Forester to let *him* ride outside. Forester hesitated, but on looking up, and seeing that there was a secure seat, with a good place to hold on, he consented. So Marco clambered up and took his seat with the driver, while the other passengers re-established themselves in the stage.

CHAPTER II.

ACCIDENTS.

Marco liked his seat upon the outside of the stage-coach very much. He could see the whole country about him to great advantage. He was very much interested in the scenery, not having been accustomed to travel among forests and mountains. The driver was a rough young man,--for the boy who drove the coach up to the door was not the regular driver. He was not disposed to talk much, and his tone and manner, in what he did say, did not indicate a very gentle disposition. Marco, however, at last got a little acquainted with him, and finally proposed to the driver to let *him* drive.

"Nonsense," said he, in reply, "you are not big enough to drive such a team as this."

"Why, there was a boy, no bigger than I, that drove the horses up to the door when we started, this morning," replied Marco.

"O yes,--Jerry,"--said the driver,--"but he'll break his neck one of these days."

"I didn't see but that he drove very well," said Marco.

The driver was silent.

"Come," persisted Marco, "let me drive a little way, and I'll do as much for you some day."

"You little fool," said the driver, "you never can do any thing for me. You are not big enough to be of any use at all."

Marco thought of the fable of the mouse and the lion, but since his new companion was in such ill-humor, he thought he would say no more to him. A resentful reply to the epithet "little fool," did in fact rise to his lips, but he suppressed it and said nothing.

It was fortunate for Marco that he did so. For whenever any person has said any thing harsh, unjust, or cruel, the most effectual reply is, generally, silence. It leaves the offender to think of what he has said, and conscience will often reprove him in silence, far more effectually than words could do it. This was the case in this instance. As they rode along in silence, the echo of the words "little fool," and the tone in which he had uttered them, lingered upon the driver's ear. He could not help thinking that he had been rather harsh with his little passenger. Presently he said,

"I don't care though,--we are coming to a level piece of ground on ahead here a little way, and then I'll see what you can make of teaming."

Marco was quite pleased at this unexpected result, and after ten or fifteen minutes, they came to the level piece of road, and the driver put the reins into Marco's hand. Marco had sometimes driven two horses, when riding out with his father in a barouche, up the Bloomingdale road in New York. He was therefore not entirely unaccustomed to the handling of reins; and he took them from the driver's hand and imitated the manner of holding them which he had observed the driver himself to adopt, quite dexterously.

The horses, in fact, needed very little guidance. They went along the road very quietly of their own accord. Marco kept wishing that a wagon or something else would come along, that he might have the satisfaction of turning out. But nothing of the kind appeared, and he was obliged to content himself with turning a little to one side, to avoid a stone. At the end of the level piece of road there was a tavern, where they were going to stop to change the horses, and Marco asked the driver to let him turn the horses up to the door. The driver consented, keeping a close watch all the time, ready to seize the reins again at a moment's notice, if there had been any appearance of difficulty. But there was none. Marco guided the horses right, and drawing in the reins with all his strength, he brought them up properly at the door; or rather, he seemed to do it,--for, in reality, the horses probably acted as much of their own accord, being accustomed to stop at this place, as from any control which Marco exercised over them through the reins.

There was, however, an advantage in this evolution, for Marco became accustomed to the feeling of the reins in his hand, and acquired a sort of confidence in his power over the horses,--greater to be sure than there was any just ground for, but which was turned to a very important account, a few hours afterward, as will be seen in the sequel.

The sailor went several times into the taverns on the way, in the course of the afternoon, to drink, until, at length, he became partially intoxicated. He felt, however, so much restrained in the presence of the passengers within the coach, that he did not become talkative and noisy, as is frequently the case in such circumstances; but was rather stupid and sleepy. In fact, no one observed that any change was taking place in his condition, until, at last, as he was coming out from the door of a tavern, where he had been in to get another drink, the driver said,

"Come, Jack, you must get up with me now, there is another passenger to get in here."

Marco, who was still in his seat, holding the reins of the horses, looked down, expecting that the sailor would make objections to this proposal,--but he found, on the contrary, that Jack, as they called him, acquiesced without making any difficulty, and allowed the driver to help him up. The new passenger got inside. Forester felt somewhat uneasy at having Marco ride any longer on the top, especially now that the sailor was going up too. But the coach was full. He himself was wedged into his seat, so that he could not get out easily. He knew, too, that two or three of the passengers were going to get out at the next stage, and so he concluded to let Marco remain outside until that time, and then to take him in again.

Marco's admiration for the sailor was very much diminished when he saw how helpless he had rendered himself by his excesses, and how unceremoniously the driver pulled and hauled him about, in getting him into his seat.

"There! hold on there," said the driver to him, in a stern voice,--"hold on well, or you'll be down head foremost under the horses' heels, at the first pitch we come to."

The poor sailor said nothing, but grasped an iron bar which passed from the top of the coach down by the side of the seat, and held on as well as he could.

They rode on in this manner for some miles, the head of the sailor swinging back and forth, helplessly, as if he was nearly asleep. Whenever Marco or the driver spoke to him, he either answered in a thick and sleepy tone of voice, or he did not reply at all. Marco watched him for a time, being continually afraid that he would fall off. He could do nothing, however, to help him, for he himself was sitting at one end of the seat while the sailor was upon the other, the driver being between them. In the mean time the sun gradually went down and the twilight came on, and as the shadows extended themselves slowly over the landscape, Marco began to find riding outside less pleasant than it had been before, and he thought that, on the whole, he should be very glad when the time arrived for him to get into the coach again, with his cousin.

At length they came to a bridge, covered with planks, which led across a small stream. It was in rather a solitary place, with woods on each side of the road. Beyond the bridge there was a level piece of road for a short distance, and then a gentle ascent, with a farmhouse near the top of it, on the right hand side of the road. At the end of the bridge, between the planks and the ground beyond them, there was a jolt, caused by the rotting away of a log which had been imbedded in the ground at the beginning of the planking. As it was rather dark, on account of the shade of the trees, the driver did not observe this jolt, and he was just beginning to put his horses to the trot, as they were leaving the bridge, when the forward wheels struck down heavily into the hollow, giving the front of the coach a sudden pitch forward and downward. Marco grasped the iron bar at his end of the seat, and saved himself; and the driver, who was habitually on his guard, had his feet so braced against the fender before him, that he would not have fallen. But the poor sailor, entirely unprepared for the shock, and perhaps unable to resist it if he had been prepared, pitched forward, lost his hold, went over the fender, and was tumbling down, as the driver had predicted, head foremost, under the horses' heels. The driver seized hold of him with one hand, but finding this insufficient dropped his reins and tried to grasp him with both. In doing it, however, he lost his own balance and went over too. He, of course, let go of the sailor, when he found that he was going himself. The sailor fell heavily and helplessly between the pole and the side of one of the horses, to the ground. The driver followed. He seized the pole with one hand, but was too late to save himself entirely, and thinking there was danger of being dragged, and finding that the horses were springing forward in a fright, he let himself drop through to the ground also. The coach passed over them in a moment, as the horses cantered on.

All this passed in an instant, and Marco, before he had a moment's time for reflection, found himself alone on his seat,--the driver run over and perhaps killed, and the horses cantering away, with the reins dangling about their heels. The first impulse, in such a case, would be to scream aloud, in terror,--which would have only made the horses run the faster. But Marco was not very easily frightened; at least, he was not easily made crazy by fright. So he did not scream; and not knowing what else to do, he sat still and did nothing.

THE ACCIDENT.

The Accident.

In the mean time, the passengers inside knew nothing of all this. Many of them had been asleep when they came over the bridge. The jolt had aroused them a little, but there was nothing to indicate to them the accident which had occurred forward, so they quietly adjusted themselves in their seats, and endeavored to compose themselves to sleep again.

The horses were well trained and gentle. They cantered on as far as the level ground extended, and then they slackened their pace as they began to rise the ascent. The idea then occurred to Marco, that perhaps he might clamber down over the fender to the pole, and then walk along upon that a little way till he could gather up the reins. Then he thought that if he could get back again with them to the driver's seat, perhaps he could stop the horses. Marco was an expert climber. He had learned this art in his gymnasium at New York; so that he had no fears in respect to his being able to get down and back again. The only danger was, lest he might frighten the horses again and set them to running anew.

After a moment's reflection, he concluded that at any rate he would try it; so he cautiously stepped over the fender and clambered down. When his feet reached the pole, he rested them a moment upon it, and clung with his hands to the fender and other parts of the front of the coach. He found his position here more unstable than he had expected; for the coach being upon springs, the forward part rose and fell with many jerks and surges, as the horses traveled swiftly along, while the pole was held in its position straight and firm. Thus the different parts of his body were connected with different systems of motion, which made his position very uncomfortable.

He found, however, after a moment's pause, that he could stand, and probably walk upon the pole; so he advanced cautiously, putting his hands on the backs of the horses, and walking along on the pole between them. The horses were somewhat disturbed by the strange sensations which they experienced, and began to canter again; but Marco, who felt more and more confidence every moment, pushed boldly on, gathered up the reins, and got all the ends together. Then taking the ends of the reins in one hand, he crept back, supporting himself by taking hold of the harness of one of the horses with the other hand. By this means he regained the coach, and then, though with some difficulty, he clambered up to his seat again.

He then endeavored to stop the horses by gathering the reins together, and pulling upon them with all his strength; but it was in vain. The horses had by this time reached a part of the road where it was more level, and they began to press forward at a more rapid pace. Marco thought of calling to Forester to get out of the window and climb along the side of the coach to the box, in order to help him; but just at that moment he saw that they were coming up opposite to the farm house, which had been in sight, at a distance, when they were crossing the bridge. So he thought that though he could not stop the horses, he might perhaps have strength enough to turn them off from the road into the farmer's yard; and that then they could be more easily stopped. In this he succeeded. By pulling the off rein of the leaders with all his strength, he was able to turn them out of the road. The pole horses followed as a matter of course,--the coach came up with a graceful sweep to the farmer's door, and then the horses were easily stopped. The farmer came at once to the door, to see what strange company had come to visit him in the stage,--his wife following; while several children crowded to the windows.

"What's here?" said a voice from the window of the coach,--"a post-office?" They thought the stage had been driven up to the door of some post-office.

Marco did not answer; in fact he was bewildered and confounded at the strangeness of his situation. He looked back over the top of the coach down the road to see what had become of the driver. To his great joy, he saw him running up behind the coach,--his hat crushed out of shape, and his clothes dusty. The passengers looked out at the windows of the stage, exclaiming,

"Why, driver! what's the matter?"

The driver made no reply. He began to brush his clothes,--and, taking off his hat, he attempted to round it out into shape again.

"What *is* the matter, driver?" said the passengers.

"Nothing," replied he, "only that drunkard of a sailor tumbled off the stage."

"Where?" "When?" exclaimed half a dozen voices. "Is he killed?"

"Killed? no," replied the driver; "I don't believe he is even sobered."

Forester and another gentleman then urgently asked where he was, and the driver told them that he was "back there a piece," as he expressed it.

"What! lying in the road?" said Forester; "open the door, and let us go and see to him."

"No," said the driver; "he has got off to the side of the road, safe. I don't believe he's hurt any. Let him take care of himself, and we'll drive on."

But Forester remonstrated strongly against leaving the poor sailor in such a condition, and in such a place; and finally it was agreed that the farmer should go down the road and see to him, so as to allow the stage-coach with the passengers to go on.

Forester was not willing, however, to have Marco ride outside any longer; and so they contrived to make room for him within. As Marco descended from his high seat, the driver said to him, as he passed him, in a low voice,

"How did you get the reins? I thought they all came down with me, under the horses' heels."

"Yes," said Marco, "they did, and I climbed down upon the pole and got them."

"Well," said the driver, "you're a smart boy. But don't tell them inside that I tumbled off. Tell them I gave you the reins, and jumped down to see the sailor."

After receiving this charge, Marco would have been under a strong temptation to tell a falsehood, if the company in the coach had asked him any questions about it. But they did not. They were so much occupied in expressing their astonishment that the sailor did not break his neck, that they asked very few questions, and after riding a short time, they relapsed into silence again. The fact that both the driver and the sailor escaped being seriously hurt, was not so wonderful as it might seem. Horses have generally an instinctive caution about not stepping upon any thing under their feet. If a little child were lying asleep in the middle of a road, and a horse were to come galloping along without any rider, the mother, who should see the sight from the window of the house, would doubtless be exceedingly terrified; but in all probability the horse would pass the child without doing it any injury. He would leap over it, or go around it, as he would if it were a stone. This is one reason why, in so many cases, persons are run over without being hurt. The driver and the sailor, however, fell rather behind the horses' heels, and escaped them in that way, and they came down so exactly into the middle of the road, that they were out of the way of the track of the wheels, and thus they escaped serious injury.

The misfortunes of the evening, however, did not end here. The road was rather rough, and there were many ruts and joltings; and one or two of the passengers seemed to feel some fear lest the stage should upset. One, who sat near the door, put his arm out at the window over the door, so as to get his hand upon the handle of the catch, in order, as he said, to be ready to open the door and spring out, at a moment's warning. The gentleman on the back seat advised him not to do it.

"If you have your arm out," said he, "the coach may fall over upon it, and break it. That's the way people get hurt by the upsetting of coaches, by thrusting out their legs and arms in all directions, when they find they are going over, and thus get them broken. You ought to fold your arms and draw in your feet, and when you find that we are going over, go in an easy attitude, with all the muscles relaxed, as if your body was a bag of corn."

The passenger laughed and took his arm in; and all the other passengers, seeing that the advice of the gentleman was reasonable, concluded to follow it if they should have occasion. And they did have occasion sooner than they had expected. For, just after dark, as they were going down a long hill at a pretty rapid rate, with a wagon a short distance before them, one of the horses of the wagon stumbled and fell, which brought the wagon to a sudden stand just before the coach. The driver perceived in an instant that there was not time to stop his horses, and that the only chance was to turn out of the road and drive by. The ground at the road-side was so much inclined, that he was almost afraid to venture this expedient, but he had no time for thought. He wheeled his horses out,--just escaped the hind wheel of the wagon--ran along by the road-side a short distance, with the wheels on one side, down very near the gutter,--and then, just as he was coming back safely into the road again, the forward wheel nearest the middle of the road, struck a small stone, and threw the coach over. The top rested upon the bank, and the horses were suddenly stopped. Sometimes, on such occasions, the *transom* bolt, as it is called, that is, the bolt by which the forward wheels are fastened to the carriage, comes out, and the horses run off with the wheels. It did not come out in this case, however. The man who had put his arm out of the window, immediately called out, in great alarm, "Hold the horses! Hold the horses! Don't let the horses run and drag us." But this vociferation was needless. A coach full of passengers and baggage is a full load for four horses, when it is mounted on wheels. It would require an exertion far beyond their strength to drag it when on its side. The horses remained quiet, therefore, while the wagoner and the driver, who was not hurt, opened the door in the upper side of the coach. The passengers then climbed out, one by one, without injury. Mary Williams came out last, with her orange-tree safe in her hand.

Chapter III.

The Grass Country.

The scene of confusion, produced by the double accident described in the last chapter, was great, but not long continued. The wagoner got his fallen horse up, and then the passengers, with the driver and wagoner, all taking hold together, soon righted the stage. None of the passengers were hurt, but the coach itself was so much injured that the driver thought it was not safe to load it heavily again. The female passengers got in, but the men walked along by the side of it, intending to travel in that way about four miles to the next tavern. Forester, however, was not inclined to take so long a walk. Fortunately, at a small distance before them, was a farmhouse which looked as if it belonged to a large and thrifty farmer. The great barns and sheds, the neat yards, the well-built walls and fences, and the large stock of cattle in the barn-yard, indicated wealth and prosperity. Forester concluded to apply here for a lodging for the night, for himself and Marco. The farmer was very willing to receive them. So the driver took off their trunks, and then the stage-coach, with the rest of the passengers, went on.

"How long shall we have to stay here?" asked Marco.

"Only till to-morrow," said Forester. "Another stage will come along to-morrow. We can stop just as well as not, as we are in no haste to get home. Besides, I should like to have you see something of the operations of a great grass farm."

Marco and Forester went into the house, and were ushered into a large room, which seemed to be both sitting-room and kitchen. A large round table was set in the middle of the floor, for supper. A monstrous dog was lying under it, with his chin resting upon his paws. There was a great settle in one corner, by the side of the fire. There were chairs also, with straight backs and seats of basket-work, a spinning-wheel, an open cupboard, and various other similar objects, which, being so different from the articles of furniture which Marco had been accustomed to see in the New York parlors, attracted his attention very strongly. Marco went and took his seat upon the settle, and the dog rose and came to him. The dog gazed into his face with an earnest look of inquiry, which plainly said, "Who are you?" while Marco patted him on the head, thereby answering as plainly, "A friend." The dog, perfectly understanding the answer, seemed satisfied, and, turning away, went back to his place again under the table.

WHO ARE YOU?

Who Are You?

One of the farmer's young men carried the trunks into a little bed-room, which opened from the great room; and then the farmer sat down and began to enter into conversation with Forester and Marco about their accident. Forester told him also about the sailor, who had tumbled off the coach a mile or two back, and been left behind. Forester said that he should like to know whether he was hurt much. Then the farmer said that he would let him take a horse and wagon the next morning and ride back and inquire. This plan was therefore agreed upon. Marco and Forester ate a good supper with the farmer's family, and then spent the evening in talking, and telling stories about horses, and sagacious dogs, and about catching wild animals in the woods with traps. About nine o'clock the family all assembled for evening prayers. After prayers Marco and Forester went to bed in their little bed-room, where they slept soundly till morning.

In the morning they were both awakened by the crowing of the cocks, at an early hour. They also heard movements in the house and in the yard before sunrise; so they arose and dressed themselves, and after attending to their morning devotions together in their room, a duty which Forester never omitted, they went out. Marco was very much interested in the morning occupations of the farm. There was the milking of the cows, and the feeding of the various animals, and the pitching off a load of corn, which had been got in the evening before and allowed to stand on the cart, on the barn-floor, over night. The cows were then to be driven to pasture, and the boy who went with them, took a bridle to catch a horse for Forester and Marco to have for their ride. Forester and Marco went with him. It was only a short walk to the pasture bars, but they had to ramble about a little while, before they found the horses. At last they found them feeding together at the edge of a grove of trees. There were two or three horses, and several long-tailed colts. The boy caught one of the horses, which he called Nero. Nero was a white horse. Marco mounted him and rode down, with the other horses and the colts following him. They put the horse in the stable until after breakfast, and then harnessed him into the wagon. When all was ready, the farmer told them to bring the sailor along with them to his house, if they found that he was hurt so that he could not travel.

When they were seated in the wagon, and had fairly commenced their ride, Marco asked Forester, what he meant last evening by a *grass* farm. "You told me," said he, "that you wanted me to see a great grass farm."

"Yes," replied Forester. "The farms in this part of the United States may be called grass farms. This is the grass country."

"Isn't it all grass country?" asked Marco. "Grass grows everywhere."

"Grass is not *cultivated* everywhere so much as it is among the mountains, in the northern states," replied Forester. "The great articles of cultivation in the United States are grass, grain, and cotton. The grass is cultivated in the northern states, the grain in the middle states, and the cotton in the southern states. The grass is food for beasts, the grain is food for man, and the cotton is for clothing. These different kinds of cultivation are not indeed exclusive in the different districts. Some grass is raised in the middle and southern states, and some grain is raised in the northern states; but, in general, the great agricultural production of the northern states is grass, and these farms among the mountains in Vermont are grass farms.

"There is one striking difference," continued Forester, "between the grass farms of the north, and the grain farms of the middle states, or the cotton plantations of the south. The grass cultivation brings with it a vast variety of occupations and processes on the farm, making the farm a little world by itself; whereas the grain and the cotton cultivation are far more simple, and require much less judgment and skill. This is rather remarkable; for one would think that raising food for beasts would require less skill than raising food or clothes for man."

"I should have thought so," said Marco.

"The reason for the difference is," replied Forester, "that in raising food for animals, it is necessary to keep the animals to eat it, on the spot, for it will not bear transportation."

"Why not?" said Marco.

"Because it is so cheap," replied Forester.

"I don't think that is any reason," replied Marco.

"A load of grass"--said Forester.

"A load of grass!" repeated Marco, laughing.

"Yes, dried grass, that is, hay. Hay, you know, is grass dried to preserve it."

"Very well," said Marco; "go on."

"A load of grass, then, is so cheap, that the cost of hauling it fifty miles would be more than it is worth. But cotton is worth a great deal more, in proportion to its bulk. It can therefore be transported to distant places to be sold and manufactured. Thus the enormous quantity of cotton which grows every summer in the southern states, is packed in bags, very tight, and is hauled to the rivers and creeks, and there it is put into steamboats and sent to the great seaports, and at the seaports it is put into ships, which carry it to England or to the northern states, to be manufactured; and it is so valuable, that it will bring a price sufficient to pay all the persons that have been employed in raising it, or in transporting it. But the grass that grows in the northern countries can not be transported. The mills for manufacturing cotton may be in one country, and the cotton be raised in another, and then, after the cotton is gathered, it may be packed and sent thousands of miles to be manufactured. But the sheep and oxen which are to eat the hay, can not be kept in one country, while the grass which they feed upon grows in another. The animals must live, in general, on the very farm which the grass grows upon. Thus, while the cotton cultivator has nothing to do but to raise his cotton and send it to market, the grass cultivator must not only raise his grass, but he must provide for and take care of all the animals which are to eat it. This makes the agriculture of the northern states a far more complicated business, because the care of animals runs into great detail, and requires great skill, and sound judgment, and the exercise of constant discretion.

"You observe," continued Forester, "that it is by the intervention of animals that the farmer gets the product of his land into such a shape that it will bear transportation. For instance, he feeds out his hay to his sheep, attending them with care and skill all the winter. In the spring he shears off their fleeces; and now he has got something which he *can* send to market. He has turned his grass into wool, and thus got its value into a much more compact form. The wool will bear transportation. Perhaps he gave a whole load of hay to his sheep, to produce a single bag of wool. So the bag of wool is worth as much as the load of hay, and is very much more easily carried to market. He can put it upon his lumber-box, and drive off fifty miles with it, to market, without any difficulty."

"His lumber-box?" asked Marco. "What is that?"

"Didn't you ever see a lumber-box?" asked Forester. "It is a square box, on runners, like those of a sleigh. The farmers have them to haul their produce to market."

"Why do they call it a lumber-box?" asked Marco.

THE LUMBER-BOX.

The Lumber-Box.

"Why, when the country was first settled, they used to carry lumber to market principally; that is, bundles of shingles and clapboards, which they made from timber cut in the woods. It requires some time for a new farm, made in the forests, to get into a condition to produce much grass for cattle. I suppose that it was in this way that these vehicles got the name of lumber-boxes. You will see a great many of them, in the winter season, coming down from every part of the country, toward the large towns on the rivers, filled with produce."

"What else do the farmers turn their grass into, besides wool?" asked Marco.

"Into beef," said Forester. "They raise cows and oxen. They let them eat the grass as it grows, all summer, and in the winter they feed them with what they have cut and dried and stored in the barn for them. The farmers are all ambitious to cut as much hay as they can, and to keep a large stock of cattle. Thus they turn the grass into beef, and the beef can be easily transported. In fact, it almost transports itself."

"How do you mean?" asked Marco.

"Why, the oxen and cows, when they are fat and ready for market, walk off in droves to Boston, to be killed. They don't kill them where they are raised, for then they would have to haul away the beef in wagons or sleighs, but make the animals walk to market themselves, and kill them there. But the farmers don't generally take their own cattle to market. Men go about the country, and call upon the farmers, and buy their cattle, and thus collect great droves. These men are called drovers. In traveling in this part of the country, late in the fall, you would see great droves of cattle and sheep, passing along the road, all going to Boston, or rather Brighton."

"Where is Brighton?" asked Marco.

"It is a town very near Boston, where the great cattle market is held. The Boston dealers come out to Brighton, and buy the cattle, and have them slaughtered, and the beef packed and sent away all over the world. Thus the farmers turn the grass into beef, and in that shape it can be transported and sold."

"And what else?" asked Marco.

"Why, they raise a great many horses in Vermont," replied Forester. "These horses live upon grass, eating it as it grows in the pastures and on the mountains, in the summer, and being fed upon hay in the barn in the winter. These horses, when they are four or five years old, are sent away to market to be sold. They can be transported very easily. A man will ride one, and lead four or five by his side. They will be worth perhaps seventy-five dollars apiece; so that one man will easily take along with him, three or four hundred dollars' worth of the produce of the farm, in the shape of horses; whereas the hay which had been consumed on the farm to make these horses, it would have taken forty yoke of oxen to move."

"Forty yoke!" repeated Marco.

"I don't mean to be exact," said Forester. "I mean it would take a great many. So that, by feeding his hay out to horses, the farmer gets his produce into a better state to be transported to market. The Vermont horses go all over the land. Thus you see that the farmers in the grass country have to turn the vegetable products which they raise, into animal products, before they can get them to market; and as the rearing of animals is a work which requires a great deal of attention, care, patience, and skill, the cultivators must be men of a higher class than those which are employed in raising cotton, or even than those who raise grain. The animals must be watched and guarded while they are young. There are a great many different diseases, and accidents, and injuries which they are exposed to, and it requires constant watchfulness, and considerable, intelligence, to guard against them. This makes a great difference in the character which is required in the laborers, in the different cases. A cotton plantation in the south can be cultivated by slaves. A grain farm in the middle states can be worked by hired laborers; but a northern grass farm, with all its oxen, cows, sheep, poultry, and horses, can only be successfully managed by the work of the owner."

"Is that the reason why they have slaves at the south?" asked Marco.

"It is a reason why slaves can be profitable at the south. In cultivating cotton or sugar, a vast proportion of all the work done in the year is the same. Almost the whole consists of a few simple processes, such as planting, hoeing, picking cotton, &c., and this is to be performed on smooth, even land, where set tasks can be easily assigned. But the work on a grass farm is endlessly varied. It would not be possible to divide it into set tasks. And then it is of such a nature, that it could not possibly be performed successfully by the mere labor of the hands. The *mind* must be employed upon it. For instance, even in getting in hay, in the summer season, the farmer has to exercise all his judgment and discretion to avoid getting it wet by the summer showers, and yet to secure it in good time, and with proper dispatch. A cotton planter may hire an overseer to see to the getting in of his cotton, and he can easily tell by the result, whether he has been faithful or not. But hay can not be got in well, without the activity, and energy, and good judgment, which can come only from the presence and immediate supervision of an owner. This produces vast differences in the nature of the business, and in the whole state of society in the two regions."

"What are the differences?" asked Marco.

"Why, in the first place," said Forester, "the fact that cotton and sugar can be cultivated by hired overseers, with slaves to do the work, enables rich men to carry on great plantations without laboring themselves. But a great grass farm could not be managed so. A man may have one thousand acres for his plantation at the south, and with a good overseer and good hands, it will all go on very well, so far as his profit is concerned. They will produce a great amount of cotton, which may be sent to market and sold, and the planter realize the money, so as to make a large profit after paying all his expenses. But if a man were to buy a thousand acres of grass land, and employ an overseer and slaves to cultivate it, every thing would go to ruin. The hay would get wet and spoiled,--the carts, wagons, and complicated tools necessary, would get broken to pieces,--the lambs would be neglected and die, and the property would soon go to destruction. Even when a rich man attempts to carry on a moderate farm by hired laborers, taking the best that he can find, he seldom succeeds."

"Does he *ever* succeed?" said Marco.

"Yes," replied Forester, "sometimes. There is Mr. Warner, who lives near my father's; he was brought up on a farm, and is practically acquainted with all the work. He has been very successful, and has a very large farm. He works now very little himself, but he watches every thing with the greatest care, and he succeeds very well. He has a great stock. He cuts fifty tons of hay."

"I should like to see his farm," said Marco.

"We'll go some day," replied Forester.

"So you see," continued Forester, "that the work of a cotton or sugar plantation, is comparatively simple and plain, requiring little judgment or mental exertion, and a great deal of plain straightforward bodily labor; while on a northern stock farm the labors are endlessly varied. Every month, every week, and almost every day brings some change. New emergencies are constantly arising, which call for deliberation and judgment. It is necessary to have a great variety of animals, in order to consume all the different productions of the farm to advantage. I can explain it all to you better, when you come to see Mr. Warner's farm."

As Nero traveled very fast, they began by this time to draw near to the place where they had left the sailor. When they came up to the house, they fastened the horse to a post, and went in. The man who lived there had gone away, but the woman said that the sailor was somewhat hurt, and asked them to come in and see him. They found him in the kitchen, with his foot up in a chair. He seemed to be in some pain. There was a great bruise on his ankle, made by the cork of one of the horses' shoes. These *corks*, as they are called, are projections, made of steel, at the heel of a horse-shoe, to give the horse a firm footing. They are made quite sharp in the winter season, when there is ice and snow upon the ground, but they are generally more blunt in the summer. This prevented the ankle's being cut as badly as it would have been, if the corks had been sharper. Forester looked at the ankle, and found that nothing had been done for it. It was inflamed and painful. He got the woman to give him a basin of warm water, and then he bathed it very carefully, which relieved the sense of tension and pain. Then he made an ointment of equal parts of tallow and oil, which he put upon the end of a bandage, and thus bound it up. This treatment relieved the poor sailor very much. Then Forester proposed to the sailor to get into the wagon and go with him to the next house, and the sailor consented. Forester was then going to pay the woman for his night's lodging, but the sailor said at once,--"No, squire, not at all. I'm much obliged to you for doing up my foot, but you need not pay any thing for me. I've got plenty of shot in the locker."

So saying, he put his hand in his pocket and drew out a handful of gold and silver pieces. But the woman, who began now to feel a little ashamed that she had not done something for the wounded foot, said he was welcome to his lodging; and so they all got into the wagon, and Nero carried them rapidly back to his master's.

CHAPTER IV.

THE VILLAGE.

In due time, and without any farther adventure, Forester and Marco arrived at the end of their journey. The village where Forester's father lived was situated in a gorge of the mountains, or rather at the entrance of a valley, which terminated at last in a gorge. There was a river flowing through this valley, and the village was upon its banks. At the upper end of the village a branch stream came in from the north, and there was a dam upon it, with some mills. The river itself was a rapid stream, flowing over a sandy and gravelly bottom, and there were broad intervals on each side of it, extending for some distance toward the higher land. Beyond these intervals, the land rose gradually, and in an undulating manner, to the foot of the mountains, which extended along the sides of the valley, and from the summits of which, one might look down upon the whole scene, with the village in the center of it as upon a map.

Marco was very much pleased with the situation, and with the appearance of the village. The street was broad, and it was shaded with rows of large maples and elms on each side. The houses were generally white, with green blinds. Most of them had pleasant yards before them and at their sides; these yards were planted with trees and shrubbery. There were also gardens behind. The mountains which surrounded the scene, gave a very secluded and sheltered appearance to the valley.

The house in which Forester lived was the largest in the village. It was a square house of two stories. It stood back a little from the road, in the middle of a large yard, ornamented with rows of trees along the sides, and groups of shrubbery in the corners and near the house. There were gravel walks leading in different directions through this yard, and on one side of the house was a carriage-way, which led from a great gate in front, to a door in one end of the house, and thence to the stable in the rear. On the other side of the house, near the street, was the office,--for Forester's father was a lawyer. The office was a small square building, with the lawyer's name over the door. There was a back door to the office, and a footpath, winding among trees and shrubbery, which led from the office to the house.

The morning after they arrived, Forester took Marco out to see the village. He intended not only to show him the various objects of interest which were to be seen, but also to explain to him why it was that such villages would spring up in a farming country, and what were the occupations of the inhabitants.

"The first thing which causes the commencement of a village in New England," said Forester, "is a water-fall."

"Why is that?" asked Marco.

"There are certain things," replied Forester, "which the farmers can not very well do for themselves, by their own strength, particularly grinding their corn, and sawing logs into boards for their houses. When they first begin to settle in a new country, they make the houses of logs, and they have to take the corn and grain a great many miles on horseback, through paths in the woods, or, in the winter, on hand-sleds, to get it ground. But as soon as any of them are able to do it, they build a dam on some stream in the neighborhood, where there is a fall in the water, and thus get a water power. This water power they employ, to turn a saw-mill and a grist-mill. Then all the farmers, when they want to build houses or barns, haul logs to the mill to get them sawed into boards, and they carry their grain to the grist-mill and get it ground. They pay the owner of the mills for doing this work for them. And thus, if there are a great many farms in the country around, and no other mills very near, so that the mills are kept all the time at work, the owner gets a great deal of pay, and gradually acquires property.

"Now, as soon as the mills are built, perhaps a blacksmith sets up a shop near them. If a blacksmith is going to open a shop anywhere in that town, it will be better for him to have it near the mills, because, as the farmers all have to come to the mills at any rate, they can avail themselves of the opportunity, to get their horses shod, or to get new tires to their wheels, when they are broken."

"Tires?" repeated Marco. "What are tires?"

"They are the iron rims around wheels. Every wheel must have an iron band about it, very tight, to strengthen it and to hold it firmly together. Without a tire, a wheel would very soon come to pieces, in rattling over a stony road.

"Besides," continued Forester, "there is a great deal of other iron work, which the farmers must have done. Farmers can, generally, do most of the wood work which they want themselves. They can make their rakes, and drags, and cart-bodies, and sleds, and tool handles; but when they want iron work, they must go to the blacksmith's. They can make a harrow-frame, but the blacksmith must make the teeth."

"Now I should think," said Marco, "that it would be easier to make the teeth than the frame."

"Perhaps it is as easy, if one has the forge and tools," replied Forester; "but the tools and fixtures, necessary for blacksmith's work, are much more expensive than those required for ordinary wood work. There must be a forge built on purpose, and an anvil, supported on a solid foundation, and various tools. All these are necessary for shoeing a single horse, and when they are all procured, they will answer for all the horses of the neighborhood. Thus it happens, that though farmers do a great deal of their wood work themselves, at their own farms, in cold and stormy weather, they generally have their iron work done at a blacksmith's at some central place, where it is easy and convenient for all of them to go."

The above conversation took place between Marco and Forester, as they were walking along together through the village, toward the part of the town where the mills were situated. Just at this moment, Marco happened to cast his eyes across the street a short distance before them, and he saw a fire on the ground in a little yard. He asked Forester what that fire could be. As soon as Forester saw the fire, he exclaimed,

"Ah! they are putting a tire upon a wheel; that's quite fortunate; we'll go across and see them."

So they left the path under the trees where they had been walking, and went obliquely across the street toward the fire. Marco saw that there was a large blacksmith's shop there. It was a very neat-looking building, painted red. There was a large door in the front, and a very low window, with a shutter hanging over it, by the side of the door. In an open yard, by the side of the shop, was the fire. The fire was in the form of a ring. There were several men standing about it; one of them, whom Marco supposed was the blacksmith, by his leather apron, was putting on small sticks of wood and chips, here and there, around the ring. Marco saw that there was a large iron hoop, as he called it, on the fire. It was not really a hoop, it was a *tire*. It was made of a much larger and thicker bar of iron, than those which are used for hoops. It was a tire belonging to a wheel. The wheel was lying upon the ground near, ready to receive the tire. It was the hind wheel of a wagon. The wagon itself was standing in front of the shop, with one end of the hind axletree supported by a block.

"What do they heat the tire for?" asked Marco.

"To swell it," replied Forester. "It is necessary to have the tire go on very tight, so as to hold the wheel together with all the force of the iron. Now when iron is heated it swells, and then shrinks again when it cools. So they heat the tire hot, and put it upon the wheel in that state. Then when it cools it shrinks, and binds the whole wheel together with a very strong grip."

"But if they put it on hot, it will burn the wood," said Marco.

"Yes," replied Forester, "it will burn the wood a little. They can not help that entirely; but they stand ready with water, to pour on, as soon as the tire is in its place, and so cool it immediately, so that it does not burn the fellies enough to injure them."

"What are the fellies?" asked Marco.

"They are the parts of the wooden rim of the wheel. The rim is made of several pieces of wood, which are called fellies."

So Forester took Marco to the wheel, and showed him the parts of which the rim was composed. While Marco was looking at the wheel, the blacksmith began to push away the burning brands a little from the tire, as it began to be hot enough. Presently he went into his shop and brought out several pairs of tongs. With these the men lifted the tire out of the fire, but the blacksmith said it was a little too hot, and he must let it cool a minute or two.

"Why, if it's very hot," said Marco, "it will grip the wheel all the harder."

"It will grip it *too* hard," said Forester. "Sometimes a tire shrinks so much as to spring the spokes out of shape. Didn't you ever see a wheel with the spokes bent out of shape?"

"I don't know," said Marco. "I never noticed wheels much."

"They do get bent, sometimes," said Forester. "It requires great care to put on a tire in such a manner, as to give it just the right degree of force to bind the wheel strongly together, without straining it."

THE TIRE.

The Tire.

As soon as the tire became of the right temperature, the men took it up again with the pairs of tongs--taking hold with them at different sides of it--and then they put it down carefully over the wheel. The wheel immediately began to smoke on all sides. In one or two places it burst into a flame. The blacksmith, however, paid no attention to this, but with a hammer, which he held in his hand, he knocked it down into its place, all around the rim; then he took up a brown pitcher full of water, which was standing near, and began to pour the water on, walking round and round the wheel as he did it, so as to extinguish the flames in every part and cool the iron. When this process was completed, Forester and Marco walked on.

"Let me see," said Forester, "where did I leave off, Marco, in my account of the growth of a village? I was telling you about the blacksmith's shop, I believe."

"Yes," said Marco.

"The next thing to the blacksmith's shop, in the history of a New England village," said Forester, "is generally a store. You see the farmers can not raise every thing they want. There are a great many things which come from foreign countries, which they have to buy."

"Such as sugar and tea," said Marco.

"Yes," replied Forester, "only they make a great deal of sugar in Vermont out of the sap of the maple-tree. We will go and see Mr. Warner's sugar bush next spring. But there are a great many things which the farmers must buy. One of the most important articles is iron. Now when a man concludes to open a store, the best place that he can have for his business is near the mills and the blacksmith's shop; because the people have to come there on other business, and so that is the most convenient place for them to visit his store. And so, by and by, when a carpenter and a mason come into the country, the little village which has thus begun to form itself, is the best place for them to settle in, for that is the place where people can most conveniently call and see them. After a while a physician comes and settles there, to heal them when they are sick, and a lawyer to prevent disputes."

"To *prevent* disputes!" said Marco. Marco had not much idea of the nature of a lawyer's business, but he had a sort of undefined and vague notion, that lawyers *made* disputes among men, and lived by them. "Why, I know," said Forester, laughing, "that lawyers have not the credit, generally, of preventing many disputes, but I believe they do. Perhaps it is because I am going to be a lawyer myself. But I really believe that lawyers prevent ten disputes, where they occasion one."

"How do they do it?" asked Marco.

"Why, they make contracts, and draw up writings, and teach men to be clear and distinct in their engagements and bargains. Then besides, when men will not pay their debts, they compel them to do it, by legal process. And there are a vast many debts which are paid, for fear of this legal process, which would not have been paid without it. Thus, knowing that the lawyers are always ready to apply the laws, men are much more careful not to break them, than they otherwise would be. So that it is no doubt vastly for the benefit of a community, not only to have efficient laws, but efficient lawyers to aid in the execution of them."

By this time, Forester and Marco had reached the part of the village where the mills were situated. Forester showed Marco the dam. It was supported by ledges of rocks on each bank, and there was a flume, which conducted the water to the wheels of the mills. There were two mills and a machine-shop. They went into the machine-shop. There was a lathe here carried by water. A man was at work at it, turning hoe handles. Forester asked him what other articles were turned there; and he said posts for bedsteads, and rounds for chairs, and such other things as were used in quantities in that part of the country. Forester asked him whether the lathe would turn brass and iron as well as wood; but he said it would not. It was not fitted for that work.

"I suppose you might have a lathe here, to work in the metals," said Forester.

"Yes," replied the man, "but it would not be worth while. There is very little of that kind of work wanted in this part of the country."

After looking at the mills, Forester and Marco walked along up the stream a little way, to look at the mill-pond. Whenever a dam is made, it causes a pond to be formed above it, more or less extensive, according to the nature of the ground. In this case there was quite a large pond, formed by the accumulation of the water above the dam. The pond was not very wide, but it extended more than a mile up the stream. The banks were picturesque and beautiful, being overhung with trees in some places, and in others presenting verdant slopes, down to the water's edge.

"That's a good pond to go a-fishing in," said Marco.

"Yes," said Forester, "and it makes fine skating ground in the winter."

Marco and Forester followed the banks of the mill-pond, until they came to the end of the still water; beyond that they saw a rapid running stream, coming down from the mountains. Marco wished to follow this stream up farther, to see what they would come to, and Forester consented. The ground ascended more and more the farther they proceeded, and the view began to be shut in by forests, precipices and mountains. Marco liked clambering over the rocks, and he found a great deal to interest him at every step of the way. He saw several squirrels and one rabbit. He wanted Forester to get him a gun and let him come out into those woods a-gunning.

"No," said Forester.

"Why not?" asked Marco.

"That is dangerous amusement."

"Why? Do you think I should get killed with my sun?" asked Marco.

"No," replied Forester, "I don't think you would; but you *might* get killed. The risk would be too great for the benefit."

"Why, you told me the other day, that it was a great thing to learn to take risks coolly. If I had a gun I could practice and learn."

"Yes," said Forester, "it is well to take risks coolly, when the advantage is sufficient to justify it. For instance, when you crept down upon the pole the other day, to get the reins, you took a great risk, but perhaps you saved the lives of the passengers by it. That was right--but to hazard your life, for the sake of the pleasure of shooting a squirrel, is not wise." Marco had before this time told him about his getting the reins.

"I shouldn't think, there was much danger," said Marco.

"No," said Forester, "there's very little danger. In using a gun, you put yourself in a very little danger of a very great calamity. There's very little probability that your gun would burst, or that you would ever shoot accidentally any other person;--very little indeed. But if the gun were to burst, and blow off one of your arms, or put out your eyes, or if you were to shoot another boy, the calamity would be a very terrible one. So we call it a great risk."

"It seems to be a small risk of a great calamity," said Marco.

"Yes," replied Forester, "but we call it a great risk. We call the risk great, when either the evil which we are in danger of is great, or when the chance of its befalling us is great. For example, if you and I were to walk over that log which lies across the stream, we should run a great risk; but that would be, not a small chance of a great evil, but a great chance of a small evil. There would be a great chance that we should fall off into the stream; but that would not be much of an evil as we should only get ourselves wet."

THE RISK.

The Risk

"Let us go and try it," said Marco. "Not I," said Forester. "You may, however, if you please. I am willing to have you take such a risk as *that*, for your amusement."

Marco went to the log and walked back and forth across it, as composedly as if it were a broad plank, lying upon the ground. Finally, he hopped across it on one foot, to show Forester his dexterity. Forester was surprised. He did not know how much skill in such feats Marco had acquired by his gymnastics in New York.

After this, Forester and Marco clambered up some rocks on an elevated summit, where they had a fine view of the village below them. They could trace the river, winding through the valley, with the green intervals on both sides of it. They could see the village and the streets, with the spire of the meeting-house in the center. The mill-pond was in full view also; and Marco's attention was attracted by a boat, which he saw gliding over the surface of the water.

"O! there is a boat," said Marco.

"Yes," said Forester. "I have paddled over the water many a time in her."

"How many oars does she pull?" asked Marco.

"Oars?" said Forester, "no oars; they use paddles."

"I wish they had some oars," said Marco, "and then I would get a crew of boys, and teach them to manage a boat man-o'-war fashion."

"How do you know any thing about it?" asked Forester.

"O, I learned at New York, in the boats at the Battery."

"Well," said Forester, "we'll have some oars made, and get a crew. I should like to learn myself."

"Let us go down and see the boat," said Marco, "now."

"No," replied Forester, "it is time to go to dinner now; but we'll come and see the boat the next time we go to take a walk."

So Marco and Forester came down the hill, and thence went across the fields home to dinner. They dined at half-past twelve o'clock, which seemed a very strange hour to Marco.

CHAPTER V.

STUDYING.

The little building where Forester's father had his office, had a small back room in it, which opened from the office proper, and which was used as a library and private study. It had a small fire place in it, and there was a table in the middle of the room, with a large portable writing-desk upon it. This desk was made of rosewood. The sides of the room were lined with book-shelves. There was one large window which looked upon the yard and garden behind. The books in this room were principally law-books, though there were some books of history and travels, and great dictionaries of various kinds. Forester conducted Marco into this room, a day or two after their arrival in the village, saying,

"Here, Marco, this is to be our study. How do you like it?"

"Very well," said Marco. "It is a very pleasant room. Am I to study all these books?"

"Not more than one at a time, at any rate," said Forester.

"*This* is my place, I suppose," said Marco; and so saying he sat down in a great arm-chair, before the portable writing-desk, which was open on the table.

THE STUDY.

The Study.

"No," said Forester, "that is *my* place. I am going to arrange your establishment near the window. James has gone to bring your desk now."

While he was speaking, the door opened, and James, the young man who lived at Forester's father's came in, bringing a desk. It was painted blue, and had four legs. These legs were of such a length as to make the desk just high enough for Marco. James put it down, at Forester's direction, near the window. It was placed with the left side toward the window, so that the light from the window would strike across the desk from left to right. This is the most convenient direction for receiving light when one is writing. Forester then placed a chair before the desk, and Marco went into the house and brought out all the books and papers which he had, and arranged them neatly in his desk. While he was gone, Forester took an inkstand and a sand-box out of a closet by the side of the fire, and filled them both, and put them on the desk. He also placed in the desk a supply of paper, in quarter sheets. After Marco had come back, and had put in his books and papers, Forester gave him a ruler and a lead pencil; also a slate and half a dozen slate pencils; also a piece of sponge and a piece of India-rubber. He gave him besides a little square phial, and sent him to fill it with water, so that he might have water always at hand to wet his sponge with.

"Now is that all you will want?" asked Forester.

"Why, yes, I should think so," said Marco. "If I should want any thing else, I can ask you, you know. You are going to stay here and study too?"

"Yes," said Forester; "but your asking me is just what I wish to avoid. I wish to arrange it so that we shall both have our time to ourselves, without interruption."

"But I shall have to ask you questions when I get into difficulty," said Marco.

"No," said Forester, "I hope not. I mean to contrive it so that you can get out of difficulty yourself. Let me see. You will want some pens. I will get a bunch of quills and make them up into pens for you."

"What, a whole bunch?" said Marco.

"Yes," replied Forester. "I don't wish to have you come to me, when I am in the midst of a law argument, to get me to make a pen."

Steel pens were very little used in those days.

While Forester was making the pens, he said,

"There are twenty-five quills in a bunch. I shall tie them up, when they are ready, into two bunches, of about a dozen in each. These you will put in your desk. When you want a pen, you will draw one out of the bunches and use it. You must not stop to look them over, to choose a good one, but you must take any one that comes first to hand, because, if any one should not be good, the sooner you get it out and try it, and ascertain that it is not good, the sooner you will get it out of the way."

"Well," said Marco, "and what shall I do with the bad ones?"

"Wipe them clean,--by the way, you must have a good penwiper,--and then put them together in a particular place in your desk. When you have thus used one bunch, tie them up and lay the bunch on my desk to be mended, and then you can go on using the other bunch. This will give me opportunity to choose a convenient time to mend the first bunch again. When I have mended them, I will tie them up and lay them on your desk again. Thus you will always have a supply of pens, and I shall never be interrupted to mend one. This will be a great deal more convenient, both for you and for me."

"Only it will use up a great many more pens," replied Marco.

"No," said Forester; "not at all. We shall have more in use at one time, it is true, but the whole bunch may last as long as if we had only one cut at a time."

"We shall begin to study," continued Forester, "at nine o'clock, and leave off at twelve. That will give you half an hour to run about and play before dinner."

"And a recess?" said Marco,--"I ought to have a recess."

"Why, there's a difficulty about a recess," said Forester. "I shall have it on my mind every day, to tell you when it is time for the recess, and when it is time to come in."

"O no," replied Marco, "I can find out when it is time for the recess. Let it be always at ten o'clock, and I can look at the watch."

Marco referred to a watch belonging to Forester's father, which was kept hung up over the mantel-piece in their little study.

"I think it probable you would find out when it was time for the recess to *begin*," said Forester, "but you would not be so careful about the end of it. You would get engaged in play, and would forget how the time was passing, and I should have to go out and call you in."

"Couldn't you have a little bell?" said Marco.

"But I don't wish to have any thing of that kind to do," said Forester, "I am going to instruct you half an hour every morning, beginning at nine o'clock, and I want to have it all so arranged, that after that, I shall be left entirely to myself, so that I can go on with my studies, as well as you with yours. If we can do this successfully, then, when noon comes, I shall feel that I have done my morning's work well, and you and I can go off in the afternoon on all sorts of expeditions. But if I have to spend the whole morning in attending to you, then I must stay at home and attend to my own studies in the afternoon."

"Well," said Marco, "I think I can find out when to come in."

"We'll try it one or two mornings, but I have no idea that you will succeed. However, we can give up the plan if we find that you stay out too long. You may have five minutes' recess every day, at eleven o'clock. On the whole it shall be *ten* minutes. And this shall be the plan of your studies for the morning. At nine o'clock, I shall give you instruction for half an hour. Then you may study arithmetic for one hour; then write half an hour; then have a recess for ten minutes: then read for the rest of the last hour. That will bring it to twelve o'clock."

"But I can't study arithmetic, alone," said Marco.

"Yes," said Forester, "I shall show you how, in the first half-hour when I am giving you my instructions. Now, are you willing really to try to carry this system into effect, pleasantly and prosperously?"

"Yes," said Marco, "I'll try."

"We shall find some inconveniences and troubles at first, I have no doubt," said Forester; "but if we are patient and persevering, we shall soon make the system go smoothly."

Forester then said, that as Marco might forget what he had to do each hour, he would make a sort of map of the hours, with the name of the study which he was to pursue marked in each. This he called a schedule. The schedule, when it was completed, was as follows:

IX. X. XI. XII. | Instruction. | Arithmetic. | Writing. | Recess. | Reading. |

This schedule was drawn neatly on a piece of paper, and fastened with wafers to the under side of the lid of Marco's desk, so that he could look at it at any time, by opening his desk.

It was in the afternoon that this conversation was held, and these preparations made. The next morning, at nine o'clock, Marco and Forester went into the little study, and Forester gave him his instructions. He took his arithmetic, and explained to him how to perform some examples, under one of the rules. Forester performed one or two of them himself, explaining very particularly all the steps. He then rubbed out his work, and directed Marco to perform them by himself in the same manner. "If you succeed in doing these right," said he, "you may set yourself some others of the same kind, with different numbers, and perform those too. If you get into any difficulty, you must not ask me, but you may set yourself sums in addition, and spend the rest of the hour in doing them. That, you can certainly do without help."

"Yes," said Marco, "I can do that."

"The next half-hour is for writing," said Forester. "I will set you some copies."

So Forester took a writing-book, which he had prepared, and wrote Marco some copies, one on the top of each page. Marco looked over him while he wrote. It is very important that a child should see his teacher write his copies, for thus he will see how the letters should be formed. Forester wrote four or five copies for Marco, and while he was writing them he gave him particular instructions about the manner of holding his pen, and shaping the letters.

"Now," said Forester, "you can not possibly have occasion to come to me about your writing; for here are pages enough for you to write upon for several days, and you have plenty of pens."

"But I should think you would want to see whether I write it well," said Marco.

"I shall examine it carefully to-morrow morning," said Forester.

"Very well," said Marco; "after the writing will come the recess."

"Yes," said Forester, "and then the reading."

"What shall I read?" asked Marco.

Forester then rose and went to one of the book-shelves, where there was a set of books, entitled the American Encyclopedia. There were thirteen octavo volumes in the set. It was rather too high for Marco to reach it, and so Forester took all the volumes down and placed them on a lower shelf, not far from the window, in a place where Marco could get easy access to them.

"There," said Forester; "there is your library. The American Encyclopedia is a sort of a dictionary. When your reading hour comes, you may take down any volume of this Encyclopedia, and turn to any article you please. Or you may think of any subject that you would like to read about, as for instance, *boat, cannon, camel, eagle, trout, horse*, or any other subject, and take down the proper volume and find the article. You can find it by the letters which are printed on the backs of the volumes."

"Let us look now," said Marco, "and see what it says about trouts."

"No, not now," replied Forester; "when your reading hour comes, you may read what you choose. Only you must have a piece of paper at hand, and write upon it the title of every article which you read, and show it to me the next morning, because I shall wish to know what you have been reading, and perhaps to question you about it. Now you understand your work, do you not?"

"Yes," said Marco; "and what are you going to do?"

"O, I'm going to study my law-books."

"Shall you stay here and study?"

"Yes," replied Forester, "I shall be here most of the time. Sometimes I shall be called into the other room, perhaps, on business with my lather; but that need not make any difference with you."

"Only, then there will be nobody to watch me," said Marco.

"O, I shall not watch you any, even when I am here. I shall pay no attention to you at all. I can judge to-morrow morning, when I come to look at your work and give you new instructions, whether you have been industrious or not.

"Even if I accidentally see you doing any thing wrong, I shall not probably say any thing about it. I shall remember it, and speak to you about it to-morrow morning, in my half-hour. I shall do everything in my half-hour."

Marco felt somewhat relieved, to think that he was not going to be under a very rigid observation in his studies.

"I do not expect," said Forester, "that you will do very well for the first few days. It will take some time to get this system under full operation. I presume that you will come to me as many as ten times the first day."

"O, no," said Marco, "I don't mean to come to you once."

"You will,--I have no doubt. What shall I say to you if you do? Will it be a good plan for me to answer your question?"

"Why, no," said Marco, "I suppose not."

"And yet, if I refuse to answer, it will not be very pleasant to you. It will put you out of humor."

"No," said Marco.

"I will have one invariable answer to give you," said Forester. "It shall be this,--Act according to your own judgment. That will be a little more civil than to take no notice of your question at all, and yet it will preserve our principle,--that I am to give you no assistance except in my half-hour. Then, besides, I will keep an account of the number of questions you ask me, and see if they do not amount to ten."

By this time Forester's half-hour was out, and Marco went to his desk.

"There's one thing," said Marco, "before I begin:--may I have the window open?"

"Act according to your own judgment," said Forester, "and there is one question asked." So Forester made one mark upon a paper which he had upon the table.

"But, cousin Forester, it is not right to count that, for I had not begun."

Forester made no reply, but began arranging his note-books, as if he was about commencing his own studies. Marco looked at him a moment, and then he rose and gently opened the window and began his work.

MARCO'S DESK.

Marco's Desk.

Marco was but little accustomed to solitary study, and, after performing one of the examples which Forester had given him, he thought he was tired, and he began to look out the window and to play with his pencil. He would lay his pencil upon the upper side of his slate, and let it roll down. As the pencil was not round, but polygonal in its form, it made a curious clicking sound in rolling down, which amused Marco, though it disturbed and troubled Forester. Whatever may have been the nice peculiarities in the delicate mechanism of Forester's ear, and of the nerves connected with it, compared with that of Marco's, by which the same sound produced a sensation of pleasure in one ear, while it gave only pain in the other, it would require a very profound philosopher to explain. But the effect was certain. Forester, however, did not speak, but let Marco roll his pencil down the slate as long as he pleased.

This was not long, however; Marco soon grew tired of it, and then began to look out the window. There was a little staple in the window sill, placed there as a means of fastening the blind. Marco pushed the point of his pencil into this staple, in order to see if it would go through. It did go through in an instant, and slipping through his fingers, it fell out of the window.

"Dear me! there goes my pencil. My pencil has dropped out of the window, cousin Forester; shall I go out and get it?"

"Act according to your own judgment," said Forester. At the same time he was saying this, he made another mark upon his paper.

"Why, you ought not to count that, cousin Forester," said Marco, "for I don't know whether you'd wish me to go and get that pencil, or take another out of my desk."

"Act according to your own judgment," replied Forester.

Marco looked perplexed and troubled. In fact, he was a little displeased to find that Forester would not answer him. He thought that, it was an unforeseen emergency, which Forester ought to have considered an exception to his rule. But he was obliged to decide the question for himself, and he concluded to go out for his pencil. It took him some time to find it in the grass, and after he had found it, he stopped for some time longer, to watch some ants which were passing in and out, at the entrance to their nest, each one bringing up a grain of sand in his forceps. When Marco came in, he found that his hour for arithmetic was so nearly expired, that he should not have time to finish another sum, if he should begin it; so he put his arithmetical apparatus away, and took out his writing-book.

Marco went through the whole forenoon pretty much in the same way. He spent a large part of his time in looking out of the window and about the room. He went out at the time for the recess, but he stayed out twenty minutes instead of ten. He was astonished, when he came in, to see how rapidly the time had passed. He then took down a volume of the Encyclopedia, and read until twelve o'clock, and then, leaving the volume of the Encyclopedia and his writing-book on his desk, he told Forester that the study hours were over, and went away.

The next morning, at nine, Forester asked him how he had got along the day before. Marco had the frankness to admit that he did not get along very well.

"Still," said Forester, "I am well satisfied on the whole. You did very well for a first experiment. In the first place, you did really make some effort to carry out my plan. You kept the reckoning of the hours, and changed your studies at the appointed time. You did not speak to me more than three or four times, and then you acquiesced pretty good-naturedly in my refusing to help you. To-day you will do better, I have no doubt, and to-morrow better still.

And thus, in the course of a week, I have great confidence that you will learn to study for three hours by yourself, to good advantage."

"Two hours and a half it is," said Marco.

"Yes," said Forester.

It resulted as Forester predicted. Marco, finding that Forester was disposed to be pleased with and to commend his efforts, made greater efforts every day, and, in the course of a week, he began to be a very respectable student. In the afternoon he used to ramble about, sometimes with Forester, and sometimes alone. He was very fond of fishing, and Forester used to allow him to go to certain parts of the river, where the water was not deep, alone, trusting to his word that he would confine himself strictly to the prescribed bounds.

CHAPTER VI.

THE LOG CANOE.

Every thing went on very prosperously, for a week or two, in the little study. Marco became more and more attentive to his studies, and more and more interested in them. He was often getting into little difficulties, it is true, and giving trouble to his uncle and aunt; but then he generally seemed sorry afterward for the trouble which he had thus occasioned, and he bore reproof, and such punishments as his cousin thought it necessary to inflict, with so much good-humor, that they all readily forgave him for his faults and misdemeanors.

One day, however, about a fortnight after he had commenced his studies, he got led away, through the influence of a peculiar temptation, into a rather serious act of transgression, which might have been followed by very grave consequences. The circumstances were these. He had commenced his studies as usual, after having received his half-hour's instruction from Forester, and was in the midst of the process of reducing the fraction 504/756 to its lowest terms, when he happened to look out of the window and to see two boys climbing over a garden fence belonging to one of the neighbor's houses, at a little distance in the rear of his uncle's house. It was a very pleasant morning, and Marco had the window open; so he could see the boys very plainly. They stopped on the farther side of the fence which they had got over, and though they were partially concealed by the fence, yet Marco could plainly perceive that they were busily employed in doing something there, though he could not imagine what. He wished very much to go and see; but he knew that it would be in vain to make request for permission, and so he contented himself with watching them.

Just at this moment his uncle opened the door which led into the little study, and asked Forester if he would step into the office. Forester did so; and then, after a few minutes, he returned, put up his books, and said that he had got to go away, and that perhaps he should not be back till noon. Marco had often been left alone at his studies for a time, but never for a whole morning before. He knew that he was to go on with his work just as if Forester had remained. So Forester bade him good morning, and then went away.

Marco watched the boys, wondering more and more what they could be doing. They kept stooping down to the ground, and moving about a little, as if they were planting seeds. But as it was entirely the wrong season for any such work, Marco concluded that they must be hiding something in the ground. "Perhaps," said he to himself, "they have been stealing some money, and are burying it. I wish I could go and see."

If there had been a door leading directly from the study into the yard, Marco would have left his studies and have gone out at once; but as it was, he could not get out without going through the office where his uncle was sitting. At last the thought struck him that he might jump out the window. He felt some hesitation at taking this step, but finally he concluded that he would do it, and just go near enough to see what the boys were hiding, and exactly where they were putting it, so that he could go afterward and find it without fail. He determined to return then immediately.

"I shall not be out longer than five minutes," said he to himself, "and I will let it go for my recess."

So he took his cap from the nail where he was accustomed to hang it, while he was at his studies, and then climbing out the window, feet foremost, he let himself down gently to the ground. He then crept slyly along through the yards and gardens, until he got pretty near the place where the boys were at work. The mystery, however, was rather increased than diminished by the near view. He could make nothing of the operations which they were engaged in; and while he was hesitating whether to go nearer, one of the boys happened to look up and spied him. Marco had intended to keep himself concealed by a tree, behind which he had taken his station, but the boy having looked up suddenly, at a moment when he happened to be off his guard, saw him before he had time to draw back under the cover he had chosen.

"Holloa, Marco," said the boy, "come here."

Marco was astonished at this frank and open invitation. He had expected that the boys, when they saw him, would have dropped at once behind the fence to conceal themselves, or that they would have caught up what he supposed they were burying, and have run away. Their accosting him in this fearless manner deranged his ideas about their probable object, and increased his curiosity to know what they were doing. So he came forth from his concealment and went toward them. When he reached the spot, the mystery was suddenly dispelled by his finding out that they were digging worms for bait, to go a-fishing.

Marco's curiosity was now changed to eager desire. The boys told him that they were going down to the river to fish for eels, and Marco's soul was all on fire to accompany them. He had never fished for eels. He knew the boys very well, and they offered to lend him a hook and line. But Marco thought that on the whole it would not do. He tried to persuade them to wait until the afternoon, but they would not consent to such a postponement of their pleasure. So Marco wished them good luck, and began to mount the fence again, with the intention of returning to his studies.

On looking toward the office, he saw his uncle coming out of the door in the rear of it, and walking toward the house. Marco immediately reflected that it would not answer for him to meet his uncle, and he descended from the fence again on the same side with the boys, until his uncle should go back. The boys thought he came back because he was undecided whether to go with them or not, and they renewed their invitations with redoubled urgency. Marco did not reply, but looked steadily toward the house. He saw a man standing in the yard with a small ladder in his hand. A moment afterward, Marco's uncle came out of the house, and, to Marco's great consternation, he perceived that he had a saw and a hatchet in his hand, and then he recollected that his uncle had been intending to prune some trees that forenoon. The trees were situated in various positions about the yard, so that Marco could neither go in at the front door of the office, nor climb in at the window, without being discovered. He did not know what to do.

In the mean time, the boys urged him to go with them. They did not know any thing about his studies, and supposed that his hesitation was only owing to his want of interest in the object of the expedition. Finally, Marco concluded to go. He supposed that he should not be able to get back into his study till noon, as he recollected that his uncle expected to be employed all the forenoon about his pruning. He thought, therefore, that his chance of detection would not be increased by staying out an hour or two longer, and so he told the boys that he would go.

When they had procured sufficient bait, they went toward the river. Their way led them not very far from the house, and they were several times in situations where they were exposed to view, in case Marco's uncle had looked toward them. Marco, however, contrived to walk by these places in such a manner as to cover himself as much as possible from view by the other boys; and besides, he hoped that his uncle was too much occupied with his pruning, to notice what boys were prowling about the village. They passed across the street in this manner, and then went down over the intervales toward the river. Marco felt quite relieved at seeing that his uncle kept steadily at his work, holding the ladder for the other man to mount by, or sawing off low branches himself, without appearing to notice the boys at all.

The river was circuitous in its course, and its banks were in some places steep, and in others low and sandy. The water was generally shallow, but in some places it was deep,--especially under the high banks. In many places there were willows and elms, overhanging the water. It was in one of these places that the boys were going to fish for eels. It was a point where the river took a sudden turn, forming a sort of angle in the stream, where the water was very dark and deep. The bank was high at that place, and it was covered with trees and bushes. Some of these trees had been undermined, and their roots and branches were floating in the water. The boys scrambled down to the brink and made ready for fishing. They cut slender poles in the bushes, for fishing-poles. There was a trunk of a tree lying along the shore, extending obliquely out a little way over the water, which furnished them a convenient footing. They stood or sat upon it, baited their hooks, and threw them over into the water. They followed the bait with their eyes as it sunk slowly down into the dark depths, among the logs, and roots, and trunks of trees, which were lying submerged in the water.

The boys remained here an hour, but they caught no eels. Either there were none there, or for some reason or other they chose not to bite. They had some talk about going to another place, but before they decided upon that plan, Marco's attention was arrested by the sight of what appeared to be a large log floating down the river. He pointed it out to the other boys, and, on closer examination, they saw that it was an old canoe, of the kind that are formed by hollowing out a log. It was not of very large size and it appeared to be rather old and decayed. Still, the boys wanted to get it very much. They gathered in their lines, and ran along the bank, keeping pace with the boat as it floated down.

BOAT ADRIFT.

Boat Adrift.

They very soon came to a reach of the river,--that is, to a length of it between one bend and another, where the water was swift and shallow. So the two boys who had been fishing with Marco threw off their shoes, and pulled up their trowsers, and ran down the bank, and into the river. The boat was far out in the stream, and they had to wade some distance before they came to it. Besides, as the boat was floating down all the time, while they were wading across, it got some distance down the stream before they could reach it. They, however, succeeded in getting it at last, and, with much floundering in the water and many shouts of laughter, they brought it over to Marco.

Marco was much pleased with the prize. It was in better condition than they had expected to find it. There was, indeed, a piece knocked out at one end, near the upper edge, but they found that it would support all three of the boys, if they sat in it carefully, and with their weight principally at the other end. For want of oars or paddles they cut poles on the banks, thinking that they could push the boat along, by planting the poles against the bottom, as the water was not deep. They drew the boat up to the shore, and poured out some water which had got into her, and then they all carefully embarked, intending to make a little voyage.

It happened that just below the place to which the boat had drifted before they overtook it, the water became somewhat deeper, and of course more smooth and still, so that it afforded a favorable place for navigating such a boat. In fact, the character of the stream, throughout its whole course for several miles, was to present a constant succession of changes, from deep and almost still water, to shallow and rapid currents, rippling over beds of sand and gravel. One of these rapids, or rips, as they were called, the boys had just passed; it being in one of them, though one more broad and less rapid than many of the others, that they had pursued and overtaken the boat. In the smooth and still water below, therefore, they had a very favorable opportunity to try their boat, for the water, though not so shallow as it was above, was still not so deep as to prevent their propelling their boat, by pushing their poles against the bottom. It required some care to preserve their equilibrium, but then the water was not deep, and they knew, therefore, that there was no danger of being drowned if they should upset.

Things went on very prosperously, until, after a few minutes, the boys suddenly found themselves drifting into deeper water. Their poles would scarcely touch the bottom. Marco, who was not much accustomed to this kind of navigation, was at first somewhat alarmed, but the other boys told him to keep quiet, and they would soon drift into shallow water again. They accordingly drew in their poles, and began to look over the edge of the boat into the water, to see if they could see any eels. They saw no eels, but the water soon began to grow shallow again, and so the boys, feeling that they were in no danger, remained quietly in their places, looking idly into the water, talking about the various objects which they saw upon the bottom.

After some minutes spent in this manner, one of the boys looked down the stream, and saw that the boat was gradually approaching another of the rapids.

"Come, boys," said he, "we must go to work, or we shall be down over the rips."

So the boys all took their poles and began to push the boat up the stream; but they found it harder than they had expected. In fact, the boat had drifted down nearer to the rapids than they ought to have allowed it to go. The water was running quite swiftly where they were, and they soon found that all their efforts were not sufficient to stem the current. The boat was carried round and round in every direction, excepting up the stream. In fact the current was rapidly acquiring the entire mastery over them, and hurrying them down to a point where the water poured on in a furious torrent through a long narrow passage between beds of stone and gravel.

"Pull, boys, pull!" said Marco; "we shall go down over the rips in spite of every thing."

The boys did pull, but they could effect nothing. The water was sweeping them along with great rapidity, notwithstanding all their struggles. Finally, when they found that they could not make head against it, so as to go up the stream, they concluded to pull for the shore. They were not in any great fear, for the river was very narrow and not more than knee deep in the rapids, so that there was no real danger of any calamity greater than getting well wet. They seemed to be also in a fair way to escape this, for they found that they could make some progress in getting their boat toward the shore. But, just as they began to think their object was about to be accomplished, they were arrested by a sudden mishap. It happened that there was a little snag in the river, nearly in the direction in which they were going. It was the end of a small log, which rose almost to the surface of the water. The greater part of the log was firmly imbedded in the sand, but there was a small portion of it which projected so far as barely to be submerged. The boys did not notice this, and, in their eagerness to run the boat ashore, it happened that they were running it across the current, just above this snag. But as the current was sweeping them down the stream at the same time that they were pushing themselves across it, it carried the boat with great force against this snag. The bottom of the boat was confined by it, while the force of the current, still pressing upon the side, overset it in a moment, and threw all the boys out into the water.

The boys scrambled out without much difficulty, and stood upon the gravelly beach. They saw at the same moment a man on the bank of the river above, who looked as if he was about to run to their aid; but when he saw that they were safe, he turned around immediately and disappeared. An instant afterward, Marco, finding that his cap was not upon his head, looked around for it, and, to his dismay, he saw it floating swiftly away down the rapids. He ran into the water and seized the boat, which was then beginning also to go away. He called upon the boys to help him pull it up and pour the water out. He then lanched it again with all speed, seized one of the poles, clambered into it, and pushed off into the swiftest part of the current, and away he went after his cap.

CAP GONE.

Cap Gone.

He resorted to this desperate measure, because he was greatly alarmed at the idea of going home without his cap. It would have certainly insured his detection, and, as he supposed, a double punishment. He now was as eager to go down the rapids as he had before been to escape them. His only care was to keep his boat head down, so that if he should encounter any snag or rock he might not be thrown broadside on. He kept a good lookout too ahead. The boat shot through the water like an arrow, and was soon clear of the rapids in the comparatively still water below.

Marco contrived to paddle with his pole, so as to overtake the cap and recover it. Then he went to the shore and landed. He drew up the boat as high as he could, and went back to seek the other boys. He concluded that it was time to go home. His conscience now began to reproach him with the wrong which he had been doing. His promised pleasure had failed. His clothes were wet and uncomfortable. His mind was anxious and unhappy. With a heavy heart he began to retrace his steps, sure of detection when he reached home, and of punishment. He did not, however, dread the punishment so much as the just displeasure which his cousin would manifest, and the evidence of the pain which he knew his cousin would suffer, when he came to learn how his pupil had betrayed the confidence which had been reposed in him. Before he set out for home, however, he took off such of his clothes as were most wet, and wrung out the water as well as he could, and then put them on again.

When he drew near to the house, he expected to see his uncle still at work, but he was not there. Marco reconnoitered the place carefully, and then went into the office. His uncle was not in the office. He passed through into the study. He was afraid that Forester would be there, but, to his surprise and joy, he was not, and there was no sign that he had been there since the morning. Marco looked at the watch, and found that it was only about half-past eleven. So he took down a volume of the Encyclopedia and began to read. He read the article *canoe*, and he found some information about the bark canoes made by Indians, but nothing about log canoes. In about fifteen minutes he heard the office door open, and his cousin Forester came in. Forester walked into the study, but said nothing to Marco. Marco kept at his work, without speaking to his cousin. He began to hope that he might yet escape. His only fear now was lest his wet clothes should be observed. He put his hand down many times to his knees, to ascertain how fast they were drying. The clothes that he wore were of woolen, and of a dark color, so that they did not show the wet very distinctly, and, besides, the sun and the air were warm that day, and the clothes had dried fast. In a word, when twelve o'clock arrived and Marco put his books away, nobody would have observed that his clothes had been wet. He ran about in the open air until dinner-time, and though, when he went in to dinner, he felt oppressed with a sense of guilt and of self-condemnation, he was satisfied that no one suspected him. Marco thought that he had had a very lucky escape.

CHAPTER VII.

A DILEMMA.

Though Marco's first feeling was that of relief, to find that he had got back from his truancy without detection, he felt, after all, ill at ease. He kept out of sight till the dinner-bell rang, and then he was almost afraid to go in, for fear that, by some accident or other, his uncle might have noticed his absence, and might ask him something about it. He was usually much interested at dinner-time in talking with Forester about plans for the afternoon; but now he felt guilty and afraid, and he was disinclined to look his uncle or his cousin in the face, or to speak a word.

And yet it was not punishment that Marco was afraid of. There were very few boys who could bear punishment of any kind with more fortitude than he, or to whom the idea of punishment gave less concern. It was the detection itself, rather than what was to come after it, that he feared. There is something in the very act of being detected and exposed in guilt, which the heart instinctively shrinks from; and many a boy would willingly bear in secret twice the pain which the punishment of an offense would bring, rather than have his commission of the offense discovered and made known.

There was, however, no indication, at the dinner table, that Marco's cousin or uncle suspected him of any wrong. They talked of various subjects in their usual manner. Forester had arranged it with Marco, to go that afternoon down to the mill-pond, to examine the boat, in order to see whether they could have it fitted with oars, and to make arrangements to that effect. Marco now hoped that Forester had forgotten this plan, and would not go. Though he had been very much interested in the plan the day before, he now felt disinclined to go. He wished to be alone, or at least out of sight of Forester. He felt as if he had a terrible secret on his mind, and that there was great danger that something or other would occur to discover it. So he hoped that Forester would have forgotten the appointment, and that it would be thus postponed to some future time.

But Forester had not forgotten it; and after dinner, he asked Marco how soon he should be ready to go. Marco said that he should be ready at any time; and in about half an hour they set out. They walked together to the mill-pond. Forester said that the boat belonged to a man who worked in the mills, but he lived a little distance above them. His house was near the water, in a little valley. The water of the pond extended up into this valley, forming a sort of bay.

THE MILLMAN'S HOUSE   The
Millman's House.

A road led to the house, but did not go beyond it. The house was small, but it had pleasant little yards and gardens about it, and various pens and coops for different sorts of animals. The man who lived there was famous for keeping a great many animals. He had pigs, and cows, and Malta cats, and two dogs,--one of them a water dog,--and ducks and geese,--among the latter, two wild geese,--and hens and rabbits; and there were two gray squirrels, hanging up in a cage by the side of the front door. Forester told Marco about these animals as they walked along.

Marco was very fond of animals, and he began to anticipate great pleasure in seeing these. When they came near the house, he ran forward to look at the wild geese. The water dog ran to meet Forester. He knew Forester, having often seen him there before. Forester and Marco rambled about the yards, looking at the animals for some time, and then went to the water's edge, which was very near the house. The ducks and geese were swimming in the water. Forester called the dog there, and Marco amused himself for some time in throwing sticks into the water, and ordering the dog, whose name was Nelson, to plunge in and go and bring them back. The boat was there too, fastened by a rope to a post in the bank. At length, after Marco had satisfied himself with these amusements, he said,

"Well, cousin Forester, here is the boat."

"Yes," said Forester, "but the man don't seem to be at home. I presume he's at the mill."

"And what shall we do in that case?" asked Marco.

"Why, I will go into the house first, and ascertain the fact, and get a paddle."

So Forester went into the house, and soon afterward returned, bringing with him a paddle. He said that the man was at the mill, but that his wife said that they might have the boat to go and find him. "I thought," said Forester, "that you would rather go in the boat than walk."

"Yes," said Marco, "I should."

"Besides," continued Forester, "I can teach you to paddle."

Marco took the paddle from Forester's hand. He had never seen one before. He said that they always used oars, not paddles, in New York harbor. A paddle is shaped very differently from an oar. It is much shorter and lighter,--though the blade is broader. A paddle is worked, too, differently from an oar. An oar acts as a lever against the side of the boat,--the middle of it resting in a small notch called a row-lock, or between two wooden pins. But a paddle is held in the hands entirely.

"What do they have paddles for in this country?" said Marco. "Oars are better."

"You are not competent to decide that question," replied Forester.

"Why not?" said Marco; "I have rowed boats many a time."

"Yes, but you have never paddled much. You have used oars, but not paddles, and so you can not compare them."

"Well," said Marco, "I mean to try this paddle now, and then I can tell."

Marco had seen the boys who were with him in the boat that morning, using their poles as paddles, and he had used one of the poles in that manner himself; and he was just upon the point of saying something upon the subject, when suddenly he recollected that it would betray him. In fact, Marco found that having such a secret as this upon his mind, was a source of great embarrassment and constraint, as he more than once came very near making some allusion inadvertently, which would have resulted in his exposure. While speaking of boats, and oars, and paddles, and such subjects, he had to be continually upon his guard and to watch all his words.

PADDLING.

Paddling.

They got into the boat and pushed out upon the water. Forester taught Marco how to use the paddle. He gave him his seat in the stern of the boat, and directed him to grasp the lower end of the handle with the other hand. Then, by dipping the blade in the water and pushing the water back, the boat was propelled forward. He also explained to him how, by turning the blade of the paddle, one way or the other, he could give the bow of the boat an impulse toward the right or toward the left.

"Thus you see," said Forester, "with a paddle you can steer, but with an oar you can not."

"With two oars I can," said Marco.

"Yes." replied Forester. "You must have two oars to guide a boat, but you can do it with one paddle. Therefore, if you can have but one, a paddle is better than an oar. There is another advantage in a paddle; that is, in using it, your face looks the way that you are going."

"Yes," rejoined Marco, "that is a great advantage."

"In rowing, you must sit with your back to the bow of the boat, and look over your shoulder to see where you are going."

"Yes," said Marco, "unless you have a steersman."

"True," replied Forester. "When you have several men to row, and one to steer, you get along very well with oars, but in case of only one man, there is an advantage in a paddle. There is still another point to be considered,--a paddle is better for a narrow boat and oars for wide ones."

"Why so?" asked Marco.

"Because," said Forester, "a certain width is required in a boat in order to work oars well. The oarsman must sit upon the seat, and extend the oar off upon one side of the boat, and there must be a certain distance between the part which he takes hold of, and the row-lock, in order to work to advantage. But it is no matter how narrow the boat is if he has a paddle, for he holds it perpendicularly over the side."

"So paddles are better," said Marco, "for one kind of boat, and oars for another."

"Yes," replied Forester, "and paddles are better for one kind of *navigation*, and oars for another. Oars require greater breadth of water to work in. In a narrow, crooked stream flowing among logs and rocks, oars would not answer at all. But with a paddle a man can worm a boat through anywhere."

"That is, if it is only wide enough for the boat to go," said Marco.

"Of course," replied Forester. "The paddle itself requires no additional space. But oars extend so far laterally"--

"Laterally?" asked Marco.

"Yes," rejoined Forester; "that is, on each side. Oars extend so far on each side, that they require a great breadth of water. If you attempt to go through a narrow place, the oars would strike."

"Why, no," said Marco. "You can give orders to trail oars."

"I don't know any thing about that," said Forester.

"That's a beautiful manoeuver," said Marco, "only it is hard to do. You see, you order them to give way hearty, so as to get a good headway, till just as you get to the narrow place, and then *trail* is the word. Then the oarsmen all whip their oars out of the row-locks in an instant, and let 'em trail alongside under the boat's counters, and she shoots through the narrow place like a bird."

Marco became very enthusiastic in describing this manoeuver, but Forester did not get a very clear idea of it, after all.

"You'll teach it to us," said Forester, "when we get our oars and a good boat's crew of boys. At any rate, a boat can be paddled continuously through a narrow space, better than it can be rowed. Therefore, paddles are generally used on rivers, where there are many narrow places to pass through. Indians and savages almost always use paddles, for they navigate many intricate and narrow passages of water."

By this time they began to draw near the mill. They landed near some great logs which were floating in the water, ready to be drawn up into the mill and sawed. They went up the bank and thence into the mill. The man who owned the boat, was tending the mill. When he wanted a log, he would take the end of a long chain down a sloping plane of planks which led to the water, and fasten it to a log. The other end of the chain was fastened round an axle in the mill, and when all was ready, the man would set the axle in motion by the machinery, and that would draw the log up. When the log was in the mill, the man would roll it over into its place, on a long platform of timber, where it was to be sawed. Then he would set the saw machinery in motion, and the platform would begin to move forward, and the saw at the same time to go up and down, sawing the log as it advanced. Thus it would saw it through, from end to end, and then, by reversing the motion of the machinery, the log was carried back again. The man would then move it a little to one side, just far enough for the thickness of the board which he wished to make, and then begin to saw again. He moved the log by means of an iron bar with a sharp point, which he struck into the end of the log, and thus pried it over, one end at a time. When the log was placed in its new position, the machinery was set in motion again, and the log was sawed through in another place, from end to end, parallel to the first sawing, leaving the width of a board between. This process was continued until the log was sawed entirely into boards, except a piece in the middle, which it was necessary to leave of double thickness, and this answered for a plank.

Marco was much interested in watching this process, and when the sawing of this log was completed, and another log drawn up into its place, Forester introduced the subject of the boat. He told the man what he wished to do, namely, to have some row-locks or thole-pins made along the sides of the boat, and some oars to row it with. It would also be necessary to have seats, or thwarts, as they are called, placed in such a manner that there should be one just before each row-lock. These seats were for the oarsmen to sit upon, in rowing. The man told Forester that he might do any thing he pleased with the boat. He was sure that Forester would do it no injury. Forester asked him who would be a good man to do the work, and the man recommended to him a wagon-maker who had a shop very near the mill.

They went to the wagon-maker and explained to him what they wanted. The wagon-maker readily undertook the work. They all went down to the boat together, to plan the seats and the places for the thole-pins. They concluded to have three pairs on each side. This would require six oars. These oars the wagon-maker promised to make, and to have all the work done by the beginning of the next week. They also concluded to have the boat taken out of the water and thoroughly calked again, and her bottom *payed* over with pitch, as she was not perfectly tight. This being all arranged, Forester and Marco began to walk toward home.

"It seems to me strange to get a wagon-maker to work on a boat," said Marco.

"In New York, I suppose you would go to a boat-builder," said Forester.

"Yes," replied Marco, "to be sure."

"There are no boat-builders here," rejoined Forester. "In fact, there are very few trades represented here, and workmen are willing to do any kind of jobs that they can."

As only a small part of the afternoon was yet passed away, Marco asked Forester if he might go down to the river a-fishing. "I can keep within my bounds, you know," said he.

"Yes," said Forester, "you *can* keep within your bounds."

"And I will," said Marco. "Don't you suppose I will?"

"Why, you can tell better than I can about that," said Forester. "You have been here now some weeks, and I have treated you with considerable trust and confidence,--have I not?"

"Why, yes," said Marco.

"I have given you leave to go a-fishing, trusting to your fidelity in keeping within your bounds. I have left you alone in your study, several times in the forenoons. I have let you go up on the mountains with other boys, and lent you my watch, so that you might know when it was time to come back. Now you can tell better than I, whether you have been faithful to all of these trusts."

Marco did not answer. He did not know what to say. He walked along in silence.

"I will leave it with you to decide," said Forester. "Here we are just home; now you may go into the study and reflect a few moments upon the subject. Call to mind all the cases in which I have treated you with trust and confidence, and consider whether you have always been faithful to the trust. If, on reflection, you think that you have, you may take your fishing-line and go a-fishing. If you feel conscious that you have at any time betrayed my confidence, you must not go this afternoon. You may go out to play wherever you please about the house and garden, but you must not go a-fishing. If you are in doubt whether you have betrayed my confidence or not, and wish to ask my opinion about some particular case which comes up to your mind, you may remain in the study till I come in, and ask me, and I will tell you. I shall be in, in a few minutes."

There was a pause here. Marco looked very serious, and walked along in silence. Such a turn to the conversation was entirely unexpected to him, and he did not know what to say.

"It is possible," continued Forester, "that you may be conscious that you have clearly been guilty of betraying the confidence which I have placed in you in some instance which I know nothing of, or which you suppose I know nothing of, and you may wish to confess it to me. If you have been guilty of any such act, the best thing that you can do is to confess it to me at once; and if you wish to do it, you may wait till I come, for that purpose. So you may wait till I come either to ask me a question, or to confess a fault. If you do not wish to do either, you may go out without waiting for me; but you must not go a-fishing unless you can truly say that you have been faithful and honest, whenever I have trusted you before."

So saying, Forester parted from Marco and went into the house. Marco slowly walked into the office, and through it into the little study. He was greatly perplexed to know what to make of this address. "Can it be," thought he, "that he knows that I went away this morning? How could he have found it out? Or did he say that, only to find out now whether I have been honest or not heretofore?"

On mature reflection, Marco concluded that Forester did not probably know any thing about his having gone away. He thought that what he had just said was only a part of Forester's general plan of managing his case, and that it did not imply that Forester entertained any particular suspicions. Marco thought that he might therefore safely go a-fishing that afternoon if he was disposed; but we must do him the justice to say, that he did not entertain the idea of doing it a moment. He determined that he would not go. But as he was not prepared to confess his fault, and as he had no question to ask, he determined to go and play about the garden. He thought a little of waiting till his cousin came in, and then honestly making a confession; but he could not quite conclude upon this, and so he determined to go and think more of it. Besides, he concluded that if he were going to make a confession at all, he should rather do it that evening when he went to bed; for Forester always came up to his room after he went to bed, to have a little friendly and serious conversation with him, and to bid him good night.

He accordingly went out before Forester came in. He spent the afternoon in a miserable state of mind. He could not divest himself of the feeling of anxiety, that in some way or other, Forester had found out his transgression. He rather wondered, that, if it were true that Forester had found it out, he had not said something to him directly about it,--but then he knew it was Forester's way not always to make known, at once, all that he knew in such cases. But then he thought, again, that Forester *could* not know any thing about it. There was no way for him to have known it. He was away all the morning, and did not come home until after Marco got back. So he concluded that Forester did not know; but he began to wish that he did. He could not bear to think of telling him, but he wished that he knew. The burden of such a secret became intolerable to him. He strolled about the yards and garden, not knowing what to do with himself, and growing all the time more and more anxious and unhappy. He was in a very serious dilemma.

Marco cast his eyes occasionally toward the office, expecting to see Forester come out. He thought Forester would want to know whether he went a-fishing or not. But he did not come. Marco spent some time in the garden with James, who was at work there raking over the ground, and gathering in such things as might be hurt by any sudden frost. Marco worked with him for some time, and endeavored to converse with him, but he did not find him very communicative, and at last he went into the house and sat on the sofa in the parlor, reading, until supper time.

Marco fully expected that Forester would ask him at supper time whether he had been a-fishing or not; but he said nothing about it. Forester told his father and mother about their plan for a boat, and gave them a full account of their visit to the mill. His mother seemed quite interested in the account, and told Marco, that, after he got his crew well trained, she should hope that he would invite her on an excursion in the boat.

"Yes," said Marco, "we will. We must have a seat, cousin Forester, for passengers and visitors, in the stern sheets."

"The stern sheets?" said Forester, "what do you mean by the stern sheets?"

"Why, it is aft," said Marco, "between the coxswain's place and the stroke-oarsman."

"You'll have to show us," said his aunt, "when we come to see the boat."

This kind of conversation somewhat relieved Marco's mind,--but still he was ill at ease, and he determined to tell Forester the whole story at bedtime, if he could only summon up courage to begin.

CHAPTER VIII.

A CONFESSION.

In the room where Marco slept, there was a large, stuffed arm-chair, which was commonly called the easy chair; it was one that was seldom used by the family, except in sickness. It stood in a corner of the room not far from the head of Marco's bed. Forester used to sit in this chair while he remained conversing with Marco, when he came up to take his light.

When Forester had taken his seat in the great chair this evening, according to his usual custom, he began his conversation by saying.

"Well, Marco, have you been helping James in the garden this afternoon?"

"Why, no," said Marco, "I did not help him much,--I don't like James very well."

"Why not?" asked Forester.

"Why, I don't think he is very accommodating," replied Marco.

"What has he done to-day, which is unaccommodating?" asked Forester.

"He would not lend me his knife. I wanted to borrow his knife to cut me a cane from some apple-tree trimmings, and he would not let me have it."

"Haven't you got a knife of your own?" asked Forester.

"Yes," said Marco, "but mine won't open."

"Won't open?" repeated Forester. "What's the cause of that?"

"Why, I suppose because the joint is rusty," replied Marco.

"How came it rusty?" asked Forester.

"Why, you see I laid it down one day on a stone, where I was at work with it, and left it there, and there happened to come a rain in the night and rusted it. I did not know where it was, and so I didn't find it for a good many days."

"Then, I presume," said Forester, "that James supposed that you would leave his knife out in the same way and spoil it."

"No," replied Marco, "that was not the reason."

"You are sure that you asked him for it distinctly, and he refused?"

"Yes," said Marco.

Here there was a moment's pause. Marco thought that his cousin Forester was considering what should be done to James, for being so unaccommodating. He did not know but that he would report him to his father and have him turned away; though Marco did not really wish to have him turned away.

But Forester said, after reflecting a moment, "That makes me think of a story I have got here; listen and hear it."

MARCO'S ROOM.

Marco's Room.

So Forester took out his pocket-book and opened it, and then appeared to be turning over the leaves, for a moment, to find a place. Then he began to read, or to appear to read, as follows:

Once there was a little girl named Anne. She came to her mother one day, as she was sitting in the parlor, and began to complain bitterly of her sister Mary. Her sister Mary was older than she was, and had a doll. Anne complained that Mary would not lend her her doll.

"Are you sure that she refused to lend you your doll?" asked her mother.

"Yes, mother, I am *sure* she did," replied Anne.

"Perhaps she is playing with it herself," said her mother.

"No," replied Anne, "she is ironing in the kitchen."

"I think you must be mistaken," said her mother. "Go and ask her again. Don't tell her I sent you, but ask her yourself, whether she really meant that she was not willing to lend you her doll."

So Anne ran off to put the question to Mary again; presently she returned with the same answer. "Mary," she said, "would not lend it to her."

"I am very sorry to hear it," said her mother, "for now I suppose I shall have to punish you."

"To punish *her*, you mean," said Anne.

"No," said her mother, "to punish you. I don't suppose *she* is to blame."

"Why, mother--how can *I* be to blame, for her not being willing to lend me her doll?"

"You *are*, I've no doubt," said her mother. "Mary is a good-natured, accommodating girl,--always ready to do kindnesses, and if she has any unwillingness to lend any thing to you, it must be that you have created it yourself, by some misconduct. So that it will prove, no doubt, that you are the one to be punished."

Here Anne began to hang her head and look a little ashamed. Her mother's supposition proved to be correct, for, on inquiring, it appeared that Mary had lent her doll to Anne a few days before, and that when she wanted it again, Anne was unwilling to give it to her, and when Mary insisted on her bringing it to her, she became angry and threw the doll out the window.

"I never heard that story before, cousin Forester," said Marco. "And I did not know that you had stories in your pocket-book."

Forester laughed and put up his pocket-book.

"I don't believe there is any story there," said Marco. "You made it up for me, I verily believe."

"Yes," said Forester, "I did. Don't it fit your case pretty well?"

"Why, I don't know," said Marco. "I don't see why he could not let me have his knife."

"Suppose *I* had asked him for his knife; don't you suppose he would have lent it to me?"

"Yes," said Marco, "I've no doubt he would; he would do any thing for *you*, of course, because you pay him--or uncle pays him, which is the same thing."

"I don't think that that is the reason altogether," replied Forester. "There was the man at the mill to-day, who said that I might take his boat and do any thing I chose to do with it."

"Yes," said Marco, "I noticed that."

"And perhaps you thought it was very much to his credit that he did so."

"Yes," said Marco.

"But the fact is," rejoined Forester, "as I think, it was more to my credit than his; because I have had his boat a great many times heretofore, and his having so much confidence in me now, shows how I have acted with his property before. I have always taken a great deal of pains to use it carefully, to bring it back to its place safely, to get the water out, if there was any in it, and leave every thing in order. I have done this, not only because it is just and right that I should not make him suffer inconvenience on account of his doing me a favor, but as a matter of policy."

"What do you mean by a matter of policy?" asked Marco.

"Why, regard to my own interest. If I did not do so, I should soon make people unwilling to lend me their things. And I think there must be some good reason why James is not willing to lend you his knife."

"Why, he says," answered Marco, "that I don't bring back his things."

"Ah!" rejoined Forester, "that's it. I thought there must be some such reason as that. You have lost your character with James, and I advise you to acquire a new one as soon as you can. Besides, you have done him injustice this evening. You represented him as refusing you his knife because he was unaccommodating and selfish, whereas it was only proper regard to the safety of his property. What you said was calculated to make an unfavorable impression on my mind against him, and one which would have been unjust."

Marco perceived that it was so, and was silent.

"I am sorry that your knife is rusty," resumed Forester. "Perhaps I can get it open for you."

"How?" asked Marco.

"Why, I believe the best way is to soak the joint in oil. The oil will insinuate itself into the joint, and then we can get hold of the blade with a pair of nippers, or something of the kind, and open it; and then, by working it to and fro a few times, the rust will work out, and the knife be as good as it was before. If it is very rusty indeed, this plan will not answer."

"What must be done in that case?" asked Marco.

"The only way then is to carry it to some kind of smith and get him to punch out the rivet. Then we can take the blade out entirely. By this means we can clean it of its rust, and then put it in again with a new rivet. If you will give me your knife to-morrow, I will try to put it in order for you again, in one or the other of these ways.

"And now," continued Forester, after a short pause, "it is time for me to go down, unless you have something which you wish to say."

Although it was not unusual for Forester to close his evening conversation in this manner, Marco's attention was particularly arrested by the excellent opportunity which this remark afforded him to make his confession. He really wished to make it,--but he did not know how to begin. He wished that his cousin would ask him something about it, or introduce the subject in some way or other, but Forester was silent. Presently he rose, came to Marco's bedside, and asked him if he was warm enough,--for the nights at this season of the year were beginning to be cool.

"Yes," said Marco, "I'm very comfortable."

"Well, then, good night." So Forester took the lamp and walked slowly toward the door.

"Cousin Forester," said Marco.

"What?" said Forester.

"Don't go just yet."

Forester turned back and advanced to the foot of the bed. There was a high foot-board at the foot of the bed, and Forester leaned upon it with the lamp in his hand.

"Is there any thing that you want to say to me?"

Marco was silent. He looked distressed and embarrassed, and moved his head restlessly on his pillow.

"There's something wrong, isn't there, Marco," said Forester, "that you are thinking whether to confess to me or not? If there is, do just as you choose about it. I like to have you confess what you have done that is wrong, but then, if you do it at all, it must be done of your own accord."

"Well," said Marco, "I want to tell you about my going away to play this forenoon."

"How long were you gone?" asked Forester.

"Pretty much all the forenoon," replied Marco.

"Well," said Forester, "I am very glad you concluded to confess it of your own accord, but I know all about it."

Marco started up in his bed and looked his cousin in the face, and said,

"Why, cousin Forester, how did you know?"

"To prove to you that I really did know, I will tell you what you did. You got out of the window soon after I went away, and went over into Mr. Eldon's garden, where George Eldon and Samuel Warner were digging worms for bait. Then you went with them down to the river. You hid behind them when you passed in sight of the house, for fear that father would see you, as he was out in the yard, pruning trees. Then you went down to the river and sat on a log under some bushes, fishing. After a while you spied an old log canoe, drifting down the river, and the other boys waded out and got it. Then you all got into it and paddled about a while, and afterward got carried over the rips and upset in the water. Your cap drifted down the stream, and you went after it in the canoe and got it. After that, you took off your stockings and wrung out the water from them, and then came home. You got into the study only about a quarter of an hour before I came."

Marco listened to this minute account of his adventures with eager interest, wondering how his cousin could have obtained so early and such complete information. After Forester had concluded, he paused a moment and breathed a long sigh. Then he laid his head down upon his pillow again, saying,

"Well, I don't see how you found it out; and I am sorry that you did, for I meant to have told you all about it myself."

Marco seemed really disappointed at having lost the opportunity to make his full confession, but Forester told him that he considered that he *had* made full confession. "You made up your mind to do it," said he, "and you did begin, and it was the beginning which required all the effort. I only refrained from asking you about the details, from a wish to show you that I really knew all about it."

"I don't see how you found it out," said Marco. "I suppose it must have been that the boys told you."

"No," replied Forester; "I have not seen either of the boys, or heard any thing from them, directly or indirectly."

"Then you must have watched me yourself," said Marco, "instead of going away."

"Do you think," said Forester, "that I would pretend that I was going away, and then just go out a little way and lie in wait to watch you?

"Why, no,"--said Marco,--"I don't really suppose that you would."

"No," said Forester, "I really went away nut of town. I went to visit a sick man and help him make his will, and I did not return until just before you saw me."

"Then I don't see how you knew," said Marco.

"It is of very little consequence to you to know that," said Forester, "but I want to ask you a little more about the affair. Are you willing to answer any question that I may ask?"

Marco said that he was, and Forester asked him about the circumstances which led him to go away. Marco explained to him how he saw the boys, and what he thought that they were doing, and what induced him to go and see them, and how he was prevented from coming back as he had intended. There was an air of openness and honesty in the manner in which Marco related these facts, which convinced Forester that he was telling the truth.

Forester was glad to find that it was not a deliberate and preconcerted plan, between Marco and the other boys, to go off on this expedition; for, bad as it was for Marco to allow himself to be drawn away by such temptations, it would have been worse, or rather it would have indicated a worse state of character, if he had deliberately planned such a truancy.

"Well," said Forester, as he was about to close the conversation, "I am very glad that you concluded to confess your fault. I am very glad, too, that you did not go a-fishing this afternoon under the sort of permission which I gave you. I infer from these two things that you wish to be cured of these faults, and to become a boy of firm moral principle. Now it is a rule with me, generally, not to punish a boy for what he confesses of his own accord. Still, I think it probable it would be better for you to have some punishment for this. It would help to make a strong impression upon your mind, and make it much more easy for you to resist such temptations in time to come. But you may decide this question yourself. If you choose to submit to a punishment, and will tell me so to-morrow morning, I will think of some suitable one for you. If you do not say any thing to me about it, I shall not punish you." So saying, Forester bade Marco good night.

The next morning, Marco met Forester on the stairs, as he was coming down to breakfast, and told him that he thought he should feel better to be punished. So Forester reflected upon the subject, and at nine o'clock, when Marco went in to commence his studies, Forester told him that he had concluded upon his punishment.

"What is it to be?" said Marco.

"It is for me not to allow you to study," replied Forester, "all this forenoon, but to require you to sit still at your desk, with nothing to do. You see it will be a sort of solitary imprisonment, only your prison will in itself be a pleasant place."

Marco thought that this would not be a very severe punishment, but he found, in enduring it, that it was in fact much more severe than he had imagined. He got very tired indeed, long before the forenoon was out. He concluded that solitary imprisonment for years, in a gloomy dungeon, must be a terrible punishment indeed.

A year or two after this time, when Marco had been entirely cured of all such faults, he one day asked Forester to explain to him how he knew where he went on this memorable forenoon; and Forester willingly explained it to him. It seems that Forester's father, though a very gentle and kind-hearted man, was a very shrewd one, and having been accustomed to the discovery, in the course of his practice, of all sorts of pranks and roguery, was less disposed to place confidence in others till he knew the confidence was deserved, than Forester himself was, who had less experience. And when he knew that Forester had gone away, leaving Marco alone, he doubted a little whether he would remain industriously at his work. While he was thinking of this, he heard a slight noise which Marco made with his feet against the clapboards of the house in getting out the window. He therefore came into the study a moment afterward, and found that Marco had gone. He looked out the window and saw him going off toward the other boys. Just at that moment the man came to help him prune his trees, but before he began this work he went into the house to James, called him to a window and pointed out Marco to him, and said,

"I want you, James, to follow him, and keep in sight of him until he returns, but if possible don't let him see you. Say nothing to me about it, but give my son Forester an account of all that you observe."

James did as he was directed, and when Forester came back he told him the whole story, just before Forester went into the study. So that Forester knew all about it, before Marco saw him. James managed the affair very adroitly, for he kept himself entirely out of sight except in one instance, and that was when the boys fell into the water. He then rushed toward them for fear that they might be drowned, but he stopped on the bank when he saw that there was no danger, and disappeared again before Marco had time to recognize him.

CHAPTER IX.

BOATING.

The alterations and improvements, which Forester had ordered in the boat, were completed at the time promised. Marco said that it would require a crew of eight to man the boat properly: six oarsmen, a bowman, and a coxswain. Marco pronounced this word as if it was spelt *coxen*. This is the proper way to pronounce it. It means the one who sits in the stern, to steer the boat and direct the rowers. In fact, the coxswain is the commander of the boat's crew.

"*I* will be bowman," said Marco, "and you can be coxswain, and then we shall want six boys for oarsmen."

"You will have to explain to me then what my duties will be," said Forester, "for I don't even know what a coxswain is."

"Why, he's the commander," said Marco. "He gives all the orders."

"Then you must be coxswain at first," said Forester, "for I don't know any thing about it. You have got to teach us all. After I have learned to manage a boat with six oars, man-of-war fashion, I should like to be coxswain sometimes very much. And it seems to me," added Forester, "that you and I had better go down first alone, until you get me taught, and then we can get the boys to come afterward."

"O no," said Marco, "you'll all learn easily enough together. I can tell you all exactly what to do."

Forester acceded to this proposal, and they made out a list of six boys, and Forester authorized Marco to invite them to come. "Be sure," said Forester, "to tell their parents that we are going out in a boat, and tell them that I am going too." Marco did this. The boys all gladly accepted the invitation. They came first to the house, and then proceeded by a path, from the foot of the garden, which led to the mill-pond. It was about half-past one when they reached the boat.

Here there was a great scene of confusion, as the boys all commenced talking and asking questions together. They found the boat in fine order, being perfectly tight and dry, and the new seats being all in their places. The oars, however, were not there. Forester recommended to Marco to send a detachment of his men, to go to the wagon-maker's shop and get them. So Marco sent off three of the boys, calculating very correctly that they could bring two oars apiece. Before many minutes they returned, each of the boys having two oars, one on each shoulder.

The other boys immediately began to take the oars, and they all advanced together toward the boat, to get in.

"Stop," exclaimed Marco, "stop, boys! you must not go aboard without an order. I'm coxswain; you must wait till I tell you, before one of you goes aboard. John, come out."

John, who had stepped into the boat, came back again on hearing this peremptory order, and the boys waited on the bank. Marco then told them to put the oars in. The boys began to pitch them in, in confusion, some falling upon the thwarts, and some into the bottom of the boat.

"No,--stop," said Marco; "that isn't the way. Put 'em in in order."

"Yes, put 'em in order," said John. "Let's put 'em in order."

"Lay 'em along the thwarts," said Marco, "the blades forward."

Marco explained to the boys how to place the oars. They were laid along the middle of the thwarts so as to leave room to sit by the side of them. They were placed in such a manner that the handle of one came upon each seat.

"*Aboard!*" said Marco, in a military tone.

The boys did not understand that order, and of course did not obey it.

"*Aboard*, I say!" repeated Marco; "when I say *Aboard*, you must all get into the boat."

With this explanation of the word of command, the boys understood what they were to do, and got aboard the boat as fast as they could. There was much confusion among them in getting their seats. Several of them began to take up their oars, until they were forbidden to do so by Marco, in a loud voice.

"You must not touch the oars," said he, "until I say *Toss*. Then you must take them and toss them right up in the air."

"How?" said one of the boys, named Joseph. "How, Marco?"

This question was scarcely heard amid the confusion.

"Be silent, boys; don't talk, and don't stop to ask *how*, but do just as I tell you."

Marco was so much accustomed to the idea which sailors attach to the word *toss*, and to the manner in which they perform the evolution, that he forgot how many different ways there might be of tossing up an oar. The proper way is, when the command is given, for each oarsman to raise the blade of his oar quick, but gently, into the air, letting the end of the handle rest upon the thwart. It is then in a position to be let down into the water conveniently when the next order, which is, *Let fall*, is given.

The raising of the oars, and then letting them fall, all exactly together, by the crew of a man-of-war's boat, makes a very pretty spectacle.

The boys, however, knew nothing about this, for Marco, as it was all very plain and familiar to him, did not realize the necessity of making very minute explanations to such new recruits as those that were under his command. Accordingly, when the order came to *toss*, some of the boys sat still, looking at Marco, and not knowing what to do; others raised their oars into the air, some one way and some another; and Joseph, who was a little discomposed by the rebuff he had met with, concluded that he would obey as literally as possible, let what would come of it and he gave his oar a high toss into the air. It fell at a short distance from him into the water, went down for a moment out of sight, and then, shooting out for half its length, it fell over upon its side and began to float away.

" TOSS."

"Toss."

Hereupon ensued just such a scene of laughter shouts, and confusion as might have been expected. All began to shout out exclamations and orders, and to give directions how to proceed to recover the lost oar. The boys whose oars were still left, thrust them confusedly into the water, and began pushing, poking, and paddling with them, in order to get the boat out to where Joseph's oar was floating. All this time Forester remained on the bank, laughing at this specimen of nautical command and subordination.

After a time the oar was recovered, and Marco, after much scolding and vociferation, got his crew in order again. Forester said that he would remain where he was, on the bank, until Marco had tried his oarsmen a little. So Marco went on giving his orders. He succeeded finally in getting the boys all in their seats again, with their oars in their hands.

"Now, boys, mind," said he, "and I'll tell you exactly what to do. *Attention!* When I say *Attention*, you must all stop talking. *Attention!* Now you mustn't speak a word. You must hold your oars out over the water and have them all ready, the handles in your hands, and when I say *Give way*, then you must all begin to row, all together exactly, so as to keep the stroke. You must keep the stroke with the stroke-oarsman."

But the boys did not know who the stroke-oarsman was, and they began clamorously to inquire, notwithstanding the injunction to silence which they had received. Marco explained to them that the stroke-oarsman was the one who sat nearest to him, that is, the one farthest aft. As the oarsmen were all sitting with their backs toward the bow of the boat, their faces were toward the stern, and therefore the one who sat farthest aft could be seen by the rest. This is the reason why the thwart which is farthest aft is made the seat of the best oarsman, and the others are required to make their motions keep time with his. For the oars in a boat that is fully manned are so close together, that, unless they keep time exactly with each other, the blades would cross and hit one another in utter confusion. But if they keep the stroke, as they call it, exactly together, all goes right. For this reason the oarsman who sits aft, by whose oar the movements of all the other oars are to be regulated, is called the stroke-oarsman.

The boys, however, knew nothing of all this. Marco contented himself with giving one general direction to them, to keep the stroke with the stroke-oarsman, and to begin when he gave the order, "*Give way.*" Accordingly, after all were silent again, the oars being extended over the water, and Forester standing on the bank watching the operation, Marco called out in the tone of command, "*Give way!*"

The boys immediately began to row, all looking at the stroke-oarsman, but failing entirely to keep time with him. The oars thumped against each other, crossed each other, and made all manner of confusion. Some could not get into the water, and others could not get out; and Joseph's oar, which somehow or other came out too suddenly, while he was pulling hard upon it, caused him to pitch backward off his seat and tumble over into the bottom of the boat.

BAD ROWING.

Bad Rowing.

"*Oars!*" said Marco, "OARS!"

What Marco meant by *oars* they did not know, so they paid no attention to the command, but some stopped rowing in despair, while others kept on, banging the blades of the oars against one another, and plashing the water, but produced no effect whatever in respect to propelling the boat. In the mean time the air was filled with shouts of laughter and loud vociferations.

"*Oars!*" exclaimed Marco again, with the voice of a colonel at the head of his regiment. "*Oars!* Why don't you stop when I say *Oars?*"

The boys began to stop, shouting to one another, "Stop!" "Stop!" In a few minutes all was still again. The boys began to take their oars in and one of them rose and said,

"Poh! this is all nonsense. You can't do any thing with oars. I'd rather have one good paddle than all the oars in New York."

In fact, Marco himself began to despair. He uttered some impatient exclamations, and tried to paddle the boat toward the shore. But he found he was almost as awkward in managing a paddle, as the other boys were in working oars. He succeeded, however, at last, in getting the boat to the shore, and then he told the boys that they might as well get out, for they could not do any thing at all about rowing.

"You don't seem to get along very well, Marco," said Forester: "what is the matter?"

"Why, I havn't got any crew. They don't know any thing about it."

"It seems to me the fault is in the commander," said Forester.

"In me?" said Marco. "Why, I ordered them right, but they wouldn't obey."

"Yes, your orders would have been right, if you had had a trained crew. But you don't manage in the right way to teach raw recruits."

"I wish you would try, then, cousin Forester," said Marco.

"Well," said Forester, "I have no objection to try. Boys, are you willing to have me for commander?"

"Yes, sir," "Yes, sir," said all the boys.

"I shall be a great deal more strict than Marco," said Forester. "So I don't expect that you will like me. But I will try. I don't want quite so many oarsmen to begin with; I should rather teach a few at a time. Are there any of you that would like to come ashore, and let the rest practice first?"

None of the boys moved. They all wished to practice first. This was just as Forester expected.

"Very well," said Forester; "I know how I can thin out my crew. As fast as I find that you don't obey my orders, I shall put you ashore."

"But suppose we don't understand?" said one of the boys.

"I shall explain fully beforehand what you are to do. And, Marco, you must observe how I manage, and then you will know another time. When you have got any thing to teach, the art consists in dividing the lesson into a great many very short steps, and letting your pupils take one at a time."

Forester knew nothing about managing a boat's crew until that day, but he had observed very attentively all the orders which Marco had given, and noticed their meaning, and thus he was prepared to manoeuver the boat as far as Marco had gone in giving his orders. He accordingly stepped into the boat and took Marco's place; while Marco himself walked forward and took his place at the bow of the boat, saying that he was going to be bowman.

"Marco," said Forester, "you say that when the order is *Attention*, the crew must be silent; what is the order when I want to give them liberty to talk again?"

"*Crew at ease*" said Marco.

"Very well. Now, boys, when I say *Attention*, you must be still, look at me, hear all I say, and obey the orders as exactly as you can, but ask no questions and give me no advice, nor speak to one another, till I say, *Crew at ease*. Then you can talk again. Perhaps two or three of you will disobey, and I have no objection to that, as I should like some excuse for putting some of you ashore."

Forester smiled as he said this, and every boy determined that he would not be the one to be sent ashore.

"*Attention!*" said Forester.

Forester then put his paddle into the water and paddled the boat out into the pond a little way. While he was doing this, there was a dead silence on board the boat. Not a boy spoke a word; and when, at last, Forester stopped paddling, the boat floated on a little way gently through the water, and not a sound was to be heard except the distant barking of a dog on the opposite shore.

"*Crew at ease*," said Forester. The boys laughed, changed their positions, and began to talk.

"I didn't get any of you ashore then," said Forester, "but I shall succeed the next time, for I shall watch my opportunity when you are all busy talking, and say, *Attention*, suddenly; then you will not all stop in an instant, but some will go on just to finish their sentence, and this will be disobeying the order, and so I shall get you ashore."

The boys laughed; they thought that it was not very good policy for Forester to give them this warning of his intention, as it put them all upon their guard. Presently the word of command came very suddenly--"*Attention!*" Every voice was hushed in an instant; the boys assumed immediately an erect position, and looked directly toward Forester.

"Joseph," said Forester, "when I give order *Toss*, you are to take up your oar and raise the blade into the air, and hold it perpendicularly, with the end of the handle resting on the thwart by your side, on the side of the boat opposite to the one on which you are going to row,--*Toss!*"

So Joseph raised his oar in the manner directed, the other boys looking on.

"Let it down again," said Forester. Joseph obeyed.

"*Crew at ease*," said Forester.

Forester acted very wisely in not keeping the attention of the crew very long at a time. By relieving them very frequently, he made the distinction between being under orders and at ease a very marked and striking one, so that the boys easily kept it in mind. In a few moments he commanded attention again, with the same success as before. He then ordered another boy to toss his oar, then another, and so on, until he had taught the movement to each one separately. He gave to each one such explanations as he needed, and when necessary he made them perform the evolution twice, so as to be sure that each one understood exactly what was to be done. Then Forester gave the command for them all to toss together, and they did so quite successfully. The oars rose and stood perpendicularly like so many masts; while Forester paddled the boat slowly through the water. Then he directed the boys to let the oars down again, gently, to their places along the thwarts, and put the crew at ease.

The boys perceived now that they were making progress. They were gaining slowly, it is true, but surely, and Marco saw where the cause of his failure was. He had not realized how entirely ignorant all these boys were of the whole mystery of managing an oar and of acting in concert; and besides, he had not had experience enough as a teacher, to know how short the steps must be made, in teaching any science or art which is entirely new.

In the same slow and cautious manner, Forester taught the boys to let the blades of their oars fall gently into the water, at the command, "*Let fall.*" He taught one at a time, as before, each boy dropping the blades into the water and letting the middle of the oar come into the row-lock, while he held the handle in his hands ready to row. Then, without letting them row any, he ordered them to *toss* again; that is, to raise the oars out of the water and hold them in the air, with the end of the handle resting upon the thwart. He drilled them in this exercise for some time, until they could go through it with ease, regularity, and dispatch. He then gave the order, "*Crew at ease*," and let the boys rest themselves and enjoy conversation.

While they were resting, Forester paddled them about. The boys asked him when he was going to let them row, and Forester told them that perhaps they had had drilling enough for one day, and if they chose he would not require any thing more of them, but would paddle them about and let them amuse themselves. But they were all eager to learn to row. So Forester consented.

He taught them the use of the oar, in the same slow and cautious manner by which his preceding instructions had been characterized. He made one learn at a time, explaining to him minutely every motion. As each one, in turn, practiced these instructions, the rest looked on, observing every thing very attentively, so as to be ready when their turn should come. At length, when they had rowed separately, he tried first two, and then four, and then six together, and finally got them so trained that they could keep the stroke very well. While they were pulling in this manner, the boat would shoot ahead very rapidly. When he wanted them to stop, he would call out, "*Oars.*" This was the order for them to stop rowing, after they had finished the stroke which they had commenced, and to hold the oars in a horizontal position, with the blades just above the water, ready to begin again whenever he should give the command.

At first the boys were inclined to stop immediately, even if they were in the middle of a stroke, if they heard the command, *oars.* But Marco said that this was wrong; they must finish the stroke, he said, if they had commenced it, and then all take the oars out of the water regularly together. Forester was careful too to give the order always between the middle and the end of a stroke, so that the obeying of the order came immediately after the issuing of it.

By this means Forester could stop them in a moment, when any thing went wrong. He would order, "*Give way,*" and then the boys would all begin to pull their oars. As soon as any of them lost the stroke, or whenever any oars began to interfere, or any other difficulty or accident occurred, he would immediately give the order, "*Oars.*" This would instantly arrest the rowing, before the difficulty became serious. Then, after a moment's pause he would say, "*Give way,*" again, when they would once more begin rowing all together. All this time, he sat in the stern and steered the boat wherever they wanted to go.

GOOD ROWING.

Good Rowing.

Marco wished to have Forester teach the boys how to back water, and to trail oars, and to put the oars apeak, and to perform various other evolutions. But Forester was very slow in going on to new manoeuvers before the old ones were made perfectly familiar. He accordingly spent nearly an hour in rowing about the pond, up and down, to make the boys familiar with the stroke. He found, as is, in fact, universally the case with beginners in the art of rowing, that they were very prone to row faster and faster, that is, to accelerate their strokes, instead of rowing regularly, keeping continually the same time. They gradually improved, however, in respect to this fault, and by the middle of the afternoon Marco began to think that they were quite a good crew. They practiced several new evolutions during the latter part of the afternoon, and just before tea time they all went home, much pleased with the afternoon's enjoyment, and with the new knowledge and skill which they had acquired. They also planned another excursion the following week.

CHAPTER X.

AN EXPEDITION.

Forester and Marco got their boat's crew well trained in the course of a week or two, and one pleasant day in September they planned a long expedition in their boat. The boys collected at the house of the owner of the boat, at one o'clock. Two of them carried a large basket which Forester had provided. It was quite heavy, and they did not know what was in it; but they supposed that it was a store of some sort of provisions for a supper, in case they should be gone so long as to need a supper. Forester carried a hatchet also.

At the proper word of command, the boys got into the boat and took their several stations. Marco took his place forward to act as bowman. It is the duty of the bowman to keep a lookout forward, that the boat does not run into any danger; and also, when the boat comes to land, to step out first and hold it by the painter, that is, the rope which is fastened to the bow, while the others get out. Marco had a pole, with an iron spike and also an iron hook in the end of it, which he used to *fend off* with, as they called it, when the boat was in danger of running against any obstacle. This was called a boat-hook.

"*Attention!*" said Forester, when the boys were all seated.

"*Toss!*"

Hereupon the boys raised the oars into the air, ready to let them down into the water.

"*Let fall!*" said Forester. The oars all fell gently and together into their places.

"*Give way!*" said Forester.

The boat began immediately to glide rapidly over the water, under the impulse which the boys gave it in rowing. "*Crew at ease,*" said Forester.

So the boys went on rowing, but understood that they had liberty to talk. One of them wished to know where Forester was going with them; but Forester said it was entirely contrary to the discipline aboard a man-of-war for the crew to ask the captain where they were going. "Besides," said Forester, "though I could easily tell you, I think you will enjoy the expedition more, to know nothing about it beforehand, but to take every thing as it comes."

Forester steered in such a manner as to put the head of the boat toward a bank at some distance from where they started, on which there was a thick forest of firs and other evergreens, growing near the water. When they got pretty near the land, he gave the order for attention, that they might observe

- 81 -

silence in going through whatever manoeuvers were required here. The next order was, *Oars*. At this the oarsmen stopped rowing, and held their oars horizontally over the water. The boat in the mean time was gliding on toward the shore.

"*Aboard!*" said Forester.

The crew then gently raised their oars into the air, and passed them over their heads into the boat, laying them upon the thwarts in their proper position, along the middle of the boat. By this order the crew supposed that Forester was going to land.

"Bear a hand, Mr. Bowman," said Forester, "and fend off from the shore."

Forester, by means of his paddle, had steered the boat up to a log which lay in the edge of the water, and Marco, at first fending off from the log, to keep the boat from striking hard, and then holding on to it with his hook, got it into a good position for landing, and held it securely.

"*Crew ashore*," said Forester.

The crew, who had learned all these orders in the course of the repeated instructions which Forester and Marco had given them, began to rise and to walk toward the bow of the boat and to go ashore. Marco landed first, and held the boat with his boat-hook, while the rest got out. Forester then ordered Marco to make the boat fast, until they were ready to embark again.

Forester then went up in the woods a little way, with his hatchet in his hand, and began to look about among the trees. Finally, he selected a small tree, with a round, straight stem, and began to cut it down. The boys gathered around him, wondering what it could be for. Forester smiled, and worked on in silence, declining to answer any of their questions. Marco said it was for a mast, he knew, but when they asked him where the sail was, he seemed perplexed, and could not answer.

As soon, however, as the tree was cut down, it was evident that it was not intended to be used as a mast, for Forester began at once to cut it up into lengths of about two feet long. What could be his design, the boys were utterly unable to imagine. He said nothing, but ordered the boys to take these lengths, one by one, and put them into the boat. There were five in all. Then he ordered the crew on board again. Marco got in last. When all were seated, the order was given to shove off, the oars were *tossed*--then *let fall* into the water. He ordered them to *back water* first, by which manoeuver the boat was backed off from the land into deep water. Then he commanded them to *give way*, and at the same time bringing the stern of the boat round by his paddle, the boat was made to shoot swiftly down the stream.

The boat went rapidly forward along the shores of the pond, and presently, on coming round a wooded point, the mills appeared in sight. As they approached the mills, they kept pretty near the shore, and at length landed just above the dam.

Forester ordered the crew ashore, at a place where there was a road leading down to the water's edge. This road was made by the teams which came down to get logs and lumber from the water. At Forester's direction, the boys drew the bow of the boat up a little way upon the land. Then he ordered the boys to take out the pieces of the stem of the little tree, and he placed one of them under the bow as a roller. The boys then took hold of the sides of the boat, three on each side, each boy opposite to his own row-lock, while Marco stood ready to put under another roller. The ascent was very gradual, so that the boat moved up easily, and the boys were very much surprised and delighted to see their boat thus running up upon the land.

It seemed to them an exercise of great power to be able to take so large a boat so easily and rapidly up such an ascent upon the land. They were aided to do it by two principles. One was the combination of their strength in one united effort, and the other was the influence of the rollers in preventing the friction of the bottom of the boat upon the ground.

Presently the whole length of the boat was out of water and resting on four rollers, which Marco had put under it, one by one, as it had advanced. Forester would then call out, "*Ahead with her!*" when the boys would move about two steps. Then Forester would give the command, "*Hold on,*" and they would stop. By this time one of the rollers would come out behind, and Marco would take it up and carry it round forward, and place it under the bow, and Forester would then say, "*Ahead with her!*" again, and the boat would immediately advance again up the acclivity.

THE PORTAGE.

The Portage.

In a very few minutes the boat was thus rolled up into a sort of a road, where the way was level. Here it went very easily. Presently it began to descend, and soon the boys saw that Forester was taking a sort of path which led by a gentle slope down to the water immediately below the mill. They were very much pleased at this, for, as they had had a great many excursions already on the mill-pond, they had become familiar with it in all its parts, and they were much animated at the idea of exploring new regions. In going down to the water on the lower side of the mill, they had, of course, no exertion to make to draw the boat, as its own weight was more than sufficient to carry it down upon the rollers. They only had to hold it back to prevent its running down too fast, and to keep it properly guided.

"It goes down pretty easy," said Marco; "but I don't see how you are ever going to get it back again."

It was, in fact, a long and rather steep descent. The boys thought that it would require far more strength than they could exercise, to bring the boat *up* such an inclination. Forester told them not to fear. He said that a good commander never put too much upon his men, or voluntarily got them into any difficulty without planning beforehand a way to get out.

They soon got down to the water's edge again. Here, instead of the broad and smooth pond which they had above the dam, they found a stream eddying, and foaming, and flowing rapidly down between rocks and logs. There was a bridge across the stream too, a short distance below. The boys were a little inclined to be afraid to embark, in what appeared to be a rather dangerous navigation, but they had confidence in Forester, and so they readily obeyed when Forester ordered the crew aboard.

"Now, Mr. Bowman," said Forester, "keep a sharp lookout ahead for rocks and snags, and fend off well when there is any danger."

So Marco kneeled upon a small seat at the bow of the boat, and looked into the water before him, while Forester propelled and guided the boat with his paddle. They advanced slowly and by a very tortuous course, so as to avoid the rocks and shallows, and at length, just above the bridge, they came to a wider and smoother passage of water: and here Forester ordered the oars out. There was only room for them to take four or five strokes before they came to the bridge, and under the bridge there was only a very narrow passage where they could go through. This passage was between one of the piers and a gravel bed. As they advanced toward it, Forester called out, "*Give way strong!*" and all the boys pulled their oars with all their strength, without, however, accelerating the strokes. This gave the boat a rapid headway, and then Forester gave the order to *trail*, when the boys simultaneously lifted the oars out of the row-locks and let them drift in the water alongside of the boat. As the boat was advancing very swiftly, the oars were immediately swept in close to her sides, and thus were out of the way, and the boat glided safely and swiftly through the passage, and emerged into a broader sheet of smooth water beyond.

"*Recover!*" said Forester. The boys then, by a peculiar manoeuver which they had learned by much practice, brought back their oars into the row-locks, and raised the blades out of the water, so as to get them into a position for rowing. "*Give way!*" said Forester, and immediately they were all in motion, the boat gliding swiftly down the stream.

After they had gone on in this way a few minutes, Forester ordered the oars *apeak*, and put the crew at ease. When the oars are apeak, they are drawn *in* a little way, so that the handle of each oar may be passed under a sort of cleat or ledge, which runs along on the inside of the boat near the upper edge of it. This keeps the oar firm in its place without the necessity of holding it, the handle being under this cleat, while the middle of the oar rests in the row-lock. Thus the oarsmen are relieved from the necessity of holding their oars, and yet the oars are all ready to be seized again in a moment, whenever it becomes desirable to commence rowing.

Meantime the boat slowly drifted down the stream. The water was here deep and comparatively still, and the boys amused themselves with looking over the sides into the depths of the water. They glided noiselessly along over various objects,--now a great flat rock, now a sunken tree, and now a bed of yellow sand. Every now and then, Forester would order the oars out, and make the oarsmen give way for a few strokes, so as to give the boat what they called steerage way, that is, way through the water, so that holding the paddle in one position or the other would steer it. In this way Forester guided the boat in the right direction, keeping it pretty near the middle of the stream.

This mill-stream, as has already been stated, emptied into the river, and the boat was now rapidly approaching the place of junction. In a few minutes more the river came into view. The boys could see it at some distance before them, running with great rapidity by a rocky point of land which formed one side of the mouth of the brook.

"Now, boys," said Forester, "is it safe for us to go out into that current?"

"Yes," said Marco, "by all means,--let us go."

"Perhaps we shall upset in the rips," said some of the boys.

"No matter if we do," said Marco; "it is not deep in the rips, and of course there is no danger."

"That is in our favor certainly," said Forester. "Whenever the current sets strong, there it is sure to be shallow, so that if we upset we should not be drowned; and where it is deep, so as to make it dangerous for us to get in, it is always still, and thus there is no danger of upsetting."

"What is the reason of that?" said one of the boys.

"The reason is given in this way," said Forester, "in the college mathematics. The velocity of a stream is inversely as the area of the section."

The boys did not understand such mathematical phraseology as this, and so Forester clothed his explanation in different language. He said that where the stream was shallow or narrow, the current must be more rapid, in order to get all the water through in so small a space, but where it is deep, it may move slowly.

Forester landed his crew upon the rocky point, where they had a very pleasant view up and down the river. He proposed to them to have their luncheon there, and to this they agreed. So they went back to the edge of the rocks, where there was a little grove of trees, and they sat down upon a log which had been worn smooth by the action of the water in floods, and bleached by the sun.

There were plenty of dry sticks and slabs lying about upon the shore, which Forester ordered the crew to collect in order to build a fire. It was not cold, and they had no need of a fire for any purposes of cooking, but a fire would look cheerful and pleasant, and they accordingly made one. Forester had some matches in his pocket. Two of the crew brought the basket from the boat, and when they had opened it, they found an abundant store of provisions. There was a dozen or more of round cakes, and a large apple-pie, which, as there were just eight of them, gave forty-five degrees to each one. There was also a jug of milk, and a silver mug, which Forester's mother had lent them for the excursion, to drink out of.

The boys, whose appetites had been sharpened by their exertions in the portage of the boat round the falls, and in rowing, did not cease to eat until the provisions were entirely exhausted, and then they carried the empty basket back to the boat. Soon after this, Forester summoned what he called a council of war, to consider the question whether they had better go down the river. He said he wanted their true and deliberate judgment in the case. He did not wish them to say what they would like, merely, but what they thought, on the whole, was best. He told them that he should not be *governed* by their advice, but, after hearing all that they had to say, he should act according to his own judgment.

"Then what's the use of asking us at all?" said Marco.

"Why, what you will say may modify my judgment. I did not say that I shall decide according to my judgment as it is now, but as it will be after I have heard what you will have to say. I shall be influenced perhaps by your reasons, but I shall decide myself. That is the theory of a council of war. The commander may be influenced by the arguments of his subalterns, but he is not governed by their votes."

Forester then called upon each of the boys, in succession, to give his opinion on the point. Marco was in favor of going down the river, but all the rest, though they said that they should like to go very much, thought it would not answer, as it would be almost impossible to get the boat up again over the rips. After the consultation was concluded, Forester said, "Well, boys, you have all given wise opinions except Marco, and his is not wise. Now we'll go aboard the boat."

"*Crew aboard!*" said Forester. The other orders followed in rapid succession: *Attention! Toss! Let fall! Backwater! Oars! Give way!* The boys considered it settled, on hearing what Forester had said of the wisdom of their several opinions, that they were now going back toward the mill; but how they were going to get the boat back above the dam they did not know, though they did not doubt that Forester had some good plan which he had not explained to them. Instead, however, of turning the head of the boat up the stream, Forester pointed it toward the river. They supposed that he was going out to the edge of the river, and that then he would turn and come back; but, to their utter amazement, he pushed boldly on directly into the current, and then, putting his helm hard up and calling out to the crew to give way strong, the boat swept round into the very center of the stream and shot down the river over the rips like an arrow.

THE EXPEDITION.

The Expedition.

"Give way, boys, hearty," said Forester. "Give way strong."

The boys pulled with all their strength, and the boat went swifter and swifter. Forester kept it in the middle of the current, where the water was deepest, though even here it was very shallow. Marco, in the mean time, who was stationed at the bows, kept a sharp lookout forward, and gave Forester notice of any impending danger. They soon got through the rips and came to the deep and still water below, where the current was gentle and the surface smooth. Here Forester ordered the oars apeak, and the crew at ease.

"We never shall get back in the world," said one of the boys; "forty men couldn't row the boat up those rips."

"Let us try," said Forester. So he ordered the oars out again, and put the boat under way. He brought her head round so as to point up stream, and calling upon the crew to give way strong, he forced her back into the rapid water. They went on a few rods, but long before they reached the most rapid part, they found that with all their exertions they could make no progress. The boat seemed stationary. "*Oars,*" said Forester. The boys stopped rowing, holding their oars in the air, just above the water. Forester then, by means of his paddle, turned the boat round again, saying, "Well, if we can't go up, we can go down stream." He then ordered the crew to give way again, and they began to glide along swiftly down the river.

The boys wondered how Forester was going to get back, but he told them to give themselves no concern on that score. "That responsibility rests on me," said he.

"But how came you to come down here," said Marco, "when you said my advice wasn't good?"

"I said your opinion was not wise. The boys who advised me not to come were wiser than you. They gave better advice, so far as they and you understood the case. But I know something which you do not, as is usual with commanders,--and therefore I came down. In view of all that *you* know, it would have been wisest to have gone back, but in view of all that *I* know, it is wisest to come down."

The curiosity of the boys was very much excited to know what it could be that Forester knew which rendered coming down the river wise; but Forester would make no explanations. He said that commanders were not generally very communicative to their crews. In the mean time the boat went on, sometimes shooting swiftly through the rapids, and sometimes floating in a more calm and quiet manner on the surface of the stiller water. In this way they went on more than a mile, enjoying the voyage very highly, and admiring the varied scenery which was presented to their view at every turn of the stream.

At one place the boys landed upon a small sandy beach under some overhanging rocks. They amused themselves in climbing about the rocks for a time, and then they were ordered aboard again, and sailed on.

Now it happened that the river, in the part of its course over which this voyage had been performed, took a great circuit, and though they had followed its course for more than a mile, they were now drawing near to a place which was not very far from Forester's father's house,--being about as much below it, as the place where the boat belonged in the mill-pond was above it. As they approached the point where the river turned again, Marco, who was looking out before, saw a sort of landing, where there was a man standing, together with a yoke of oxen. It was just sunset when they approached this spot. When they arrived at it, the whole mystery was explained, for they found that the man was James, who lived at Forester's father's, and the oxen were his father's oxen. James had come down, under an appointment which Forester had secretly made with him, with the oxen and a drag, and by means of them he hauled the boat across to the mill-pond again, by a back road which led directly across the pastures, and lanched it safely again into the water close to the dwelling of its owner. So the boys had, as it were, the pleasure of sliding down hill, without the labor of drawing their sleds up again.

THE DRAG.

The Drag.

Marco was very much pleased with this expedition. Forester told him when they got home, that the Indians often carried their canoes around falls, or from one river to another, and that such carrying-places were called *portages*.

CHAPTER XI.

LOST IN THE WOODS.

While Marco Paul was in Vermont, he and Forester had a remarkable adventure in the woods. They got lost in fact, and for a time it seemed quite doubtful how they were ever to find their way home. It happened thus.

One morning in the fall of the year, Marco, walking along toward the barn with James, asked James what he was going to do that day.

"I expect that I am going to gather apples," said James.

"Well," said Marco. "Are you going in the cart?"

"Yes," said James.

"And may I go with you?" asked Marco.

"Yes," said James.

"And help gather the apples? said Marco.

"Yes," said James.

"And drive the oxen a little way?" asked Marco.

"Yes," said James.

"Well." said Marco. "I will run and get my goad-stick."

Marco went toward the house intending to go in and get his goad-stick. On his way he met his uncle. His uncle asked him whether James was out in the barn. Marco said that he was, and his uncle then asked him to go and request James to come to him. Marco did so, and he and James then came along toward the house together.

Marco's uncle stood upon the step of the door.

"James," said he, "I was thinking that we ought to send for the horses;--and the apples ought to be gathered too. Which is it best to do?"

"I hardly know, sir," said James. "It is high time that the apples were gathered, and yet we promised to send for the horses to-day."

"I can go and get the horses," said Marco,--"just as well as not. Where is it?"

"Oh no," said his uncle. "It is ten or fifteen miles from here. Isn't it, James?"

"Yes," said James, "by the road. I suppose it is about *four* miles through the woods. I was intending to walk there, through the woods, and then to come home round by the road. It is rather a rough road for horses through the woods."

"Let cousin Forester and me go," said Marco. "I will go and ask him."

So Marco went and found Forester. When Forester heard of the plan he was quite inclined to accede to it. He had been much engaged in studying for some time, and had had very little exercise and recreation, so that he was easily persuaded to undertake an expedition. The plan was all soon agreed upon. The horses had been put out to pasture at a farmer's up the river about twelve miles. In going that twelve miles the river took a great turn, so that in fact the farm where the horses were pastured was not, in a straight line, more than four miles from Mr. Forester's house. But the intermediate country was a desolate and almost impassable region of forests and mountains. There was, indeed, a sort of footpath by which it was possible for men to get through, but this path was dangerous, and in fact almost impracticable for horses. So James had formed the plan of walking through the woods by the path, and then of coming home by the road, riding one of the horses and leading the other.

Forester and Marco concluded to adopt the same plan; except that in coming home there would be just a horse a-piece for them to ride. They put up some provisions to eat on the way, packing them in Marco's knapsack. The knapsack, when it was ready, was strapped upon Marco's back, for he insisted on carrying it. Forester consented to this arrangement, secretly intending, however, not to allow Marco to carry the load very far.

Forester asked James if there would be any difficulty about the way. James said that there would not be. The path, though it was not an easy one to travel, was very easy to find.

"You go on," said he, "along the back road about three quarters of a mile, and then you will come to a small school-house on the left hand side of the road, on a sort of hill. It is in the Jones district."

"What sort of a school-house is it?" asked Forester.

"It is a small school-house, with a little cupola upon the top of it," said James, "for a bell. It stands upon a knoll by the side of the road. Just beyond it the main road turns to the right, and there is a narrower road leading off to the left through a gate. You must go through that gate and then follow the path into the woods."

"We can find it, I think," said Forester.

"Yes," said Marco, "I know the place very well."

Forester said he thought that they should find the way without any difficulty, and so bidding his uncle and aunt good-bye, he and Marco set out.

They went through the garden, and from the garden they passed out through a small gate into the orchard. Marco wished to go this way in order to get some apples. He chose two from off his favorite tree and put them into the knapsack, and took another in his hand to eat by the way. Forester did the same, only he put the two that he carried with him, into his pockets.

From the orchard the travelers walked across a field and down into the glen, and after crossing a brook upon some stepping-stones, they ascended upon the other side, and presently climbing over a fence, they came out into what James had called the back road. They walked along upon this road, for about three quarters of a mile, until at last they came in sight of the school-house. Marco spied it first.

"There," said Marco, "that is the school-house."

"How do you know that that is the one?" asked Forester.

"Oh, I know the Jones district very well," said Marco.

In New England the tract of country included within the jurisdiction of a town, is divided into districts for the establishment and support of schools. These districts are called school-districts, and each one is generally named from some of the principal families that happen to live in it. It happened that there were several families of the name of Jones that lived in this part of the town, and so their district was called the Jones district.

"How do you happen to know it?" said Forester.

"Oh, I came out here two or three times with Thomas Jones to set my squirrel trap," said Marco. "There goes Thomas Jones now."

"Where?" asked Forester.

"There," said Marco, pointing along the road a little way.

Forester looked forward, and saw in the road before them a boy walking toward the school-house, with his slate under his arm. Beyond the boy, upon the knoll on the left side of the road, was the school-house itself.

THE SCHOOL-HOUSE.

The School-House.

The school-house was not far from the road, and there was a little grove of trees behind it. Beyond the school-house, and almost directly before them, Marco and Forester saw the road turning a little to the left toward the gate.

"There is the gate," said Marco, "that we are to go through."

"Yes," said Forester, "that must be the one."

Forester and Marco walked on until they came to the school-house. Thomas got to the school-house before them, and went in. Forester and Marco passed on and went through the gate. They then went on beyond the gate a little way till they came to a pair of bars. Marco took down all but the topmost bar, and Forester, stooping down, passed under. Marco attempted to do the same; but forgetting that he had a knapsack upon his back, he did not stoop low enough, and gave his knapsack such a knock as almost threw him down. Fortunately there was nothing frangible inside, and so no damage was done. One of his apples was mellowed a little; that was all.

The path led the travelers first across a rough and rocky pasture, and then it suddenly entered a wood where every thing wore an expression of wild and solemn grandeur. The trees were very lofty, and consisted of tall stems, rising to a vast height and surmounted above with a tuft of branches, which together formed a broad canopy over the heads of the travelers, and produced a sort of somber twilight below. Birds sang in plaintive notes on the tops of distant trees, and now and then a squirrel was seen running along the ground, or climbing up the trunk of some vast hemlock or pine.

"I hope that we shall not lose our way in these woods," said Forester.

"Oh, there is no danger of that," rejoined Marco. "The path is very plain."

"It seems plain here," said Forester, "and I presume that there can not be any danger, or James would have recommended to us to go the other way."

"We shall come home the other way," said Marco. "I wonder if there are any saddles. Twelve miles would be too far to ride bareback."

"Yes," said Forester, "there are saddles. I asked James about that."

The path which Forester and Marco were pursuing soon began to ascend. It ascended at first gradually, and afterward more and more precipitously, and at length began to wind about among rocks and precipices in such a manner, that Marco said he did not wonder at all that James said it would be a rough road for horses.

"I think it is a very rough road for boys," said Forester.

"Boys?" repeated Marco. "Do you call yourself boys."

"For *men* then," said Forester.

"But *I* am not a man," said Marco.

"Then I don't see how I can express my idea," said Forester.

Marco's attention was here diverted from the rhetorical difficulty in which Forester had become involved, by a very deep chasm upon one side of the path. He went to the brink of it and could hear the roaring of a torrent far below.

"I mean to throw a stone down," said Marco. He accordingly, after looking around for a moment, found a stone about as large as his head. This stone he contrived to bring to the edge of the precipice and then to throw it over. It went thundering down among the rocks and trees below, while Marco stood upon the brink and listened to the sound of the echoes and reverberations. He then got another stone larger than the first, and threw that down; after which he and Forester resumed their journey.

The path, though it was a very rough and tortuous one, was pretty plain; and it is probable that the travelers would have found no difficulty in following it to the end of their route, had it not been for an occurrence which they had not at all anticipated, but which was one, nevertheless, that has often taken place to confuse the steps of mountain travelers and make them lose their way. This occurrence was a fall of snow.

It was not late enough in the year for snow upon the lowlands, but snow falls very early in the autumn upon the summits of mountains. Marco and Forester had not anticipated stormy weather of any kind, when they left home; for the wind was west and the sky was clear. When, however, they had accomplished about one half of their journey, large masses of fleecy clouds began to drive over the mountains, and presently, all at once, it began to snow. Marco was extremely delighted to see the snow falling. Forester was not so much pleased. On the other hand, he looked somewhat concerned. He did not at first think how the snow could do them any serious injury, but he seemed to have an undefined sense of danger from it, and appeared uneasy. They both, however, walked on.

The region through which the path led at the time when the snow came on, was a tract of flat land on the summit of the mountainous range, with small and scattered trees here and there upon it. The best thing, probably, for the travelers to have done in the emergency would have been to have turned round the moment it began to snow, and go back as fast as possible by the way that they came, as long as they were sure of the path, and then to wait until the fallen snow had melted. If they found then that the snow did not melt, so that they could see the path again, it would be better to return altogether, as their chance of being able to follow the path back toward their home would be much greater than that of pursuing it forward; for they might expect to find some guidance, in going back, by their recognition of the place which they had passed in ascending.

Forester, however, did not happen to think of this; and so when it began to snow, his only immediate desire was to go forward as fast as possible, so as to get into the woods again where he and Marco would be in some measure under shelter.

Marco finding that Forester appeared somewhat anxious, began to feel some sentiment of fear himself.

"Who would have thought," said he, "that we should have got caught out in this snow-storm?"

"Oh, it is not a snow-storm," replied Forester. "It is only a little snow flurry. It will be over in a few minutes."

"How do you know that it is not going to be a snow-storm?" asked Marco.

"Because storms never come out of the west," replied Forester.

It snowed, however, faster and faster, and the ground soon began to be entirely whitened. Forester pressed on, but he soon found himself at a loss for his way. The air was so filled with the descending flakes, that he could see only a very short distance before him. The view of the forests and mountains was cut off on every side, and nothing presented itself to the eye but the dim forms of the rocks and trees which were near. These, too, were indistinct and shapeless. The ground was soon entirely covered, and all hope of finding the path entirely disappeared. Forester went back then a short distance, endeavoring to retrace his steps. He followed the foot-prints a little way, but all traces of them were soon obliterated. When he found that the steps could no longer be seen, he went toward a tree which he saw rising dimly at a little distance before him. The tree proved to be a large hemlock, with wide-spreading branches. There was a place under this tree where the ground was bare, having been sheltered from the snow by the branches of the tree. There were some rocks too lying under this tree. Forester walked up to them and sat down. Marco followed his example.

"Well, Marco," said Forester, "we are really lost."

"And what are we going to do?" asked Marco, with a countenance of great concern.

"The first thing is," said Forester, "to open the knapsack, and see what there is inside that is good to eat."

So Forester took the knapsack off from his shoulders,--for he had taken it from Marco some time before, and laying it upon a large flat stone by his side, he began to open it, and to take out the provisions.

Forester was afraid that he and Marco had got themselves into somewhat serious difficulty, but he wished to teach Marco that in emergencies of such a nature, it would do no good to give way to a panic, or to unnecessary anxiety. So he assumed an unconcerned and contented air, and made arrangements for the luncheon, just as if they had stopped there to eat it of their own accord, and without being in any difficulty whatever about the prosecution of the journey.

Marco, however, seemed to be quite uneasy.

"What are we going to do?" said he. "If we get lost in this snow-storm, we shall have to stay in the woods perhaps all night."

"Yes," said Forester, "that we can do. We have done that before."

Forester here alluded to an occasion on which he and Marco had spent the night in a hut in the woods, when traveling in Maine.

"But we had an axe then," said Marco, "to make a camp."

"Yes," replied Forester, "that is true. I don't think, however, that we shall have to stay in the woods all night now. We have *three* chances for avoiding it."

"What are the three?" said Marco.

"Why, in the first place," replied Forester, "we can stay where we are until it stops snowing,--in fact it has almost stopped now. Then I presume that the sun will come out, and in half an hour melt away all the snow. Then we can find our path again, and go on."

"But I don't think it is certain that we can find our path again," said Marco.

"Nor do I," said Forester, "but there's a chance of it. I did not say that we had three certainties, but three chances."

"Well," said Marco; "go on; what are the other two?"

"If we can not find the path," said Forester, "either because the snow does not melt, or for any other reason, then we can remain where we are until night, and the people, finding that we do not come home, will send up for us."

"And how can they find us?" asked Marco.

"Why, they will come up the path, of course, and we can not be very far from the path, for we only lost it a few minutes before we came here. Of course they will come up very near to this place;--and they will come shouting out, every few minutes, as loud as they can, and so we shall hear them."

"Yes," said Marco, "I see; that is a pretty good chance."

"The third chance for us," said Forester, "is to go down into the first glen or valley that we can find, and then we shall probably come to a stream. Then we can follow the stream down to the river."

"How do you know that it goes to the river?" asked Marco.

"All mountain streams do, of course," said Forester. "They go down wherever they can find a valley or a hollow,--joining together and taking in branches as they proceed,--until they get down into the level country, and then they flow to the nearest river, and so to the sea. Now I know that the river takes a bend around this mountainous tract, and almost surrounds it, and all the streams from it must flow into the river without going very far. We could follow one down, though we should probably find the way very rough and difficult."

"Let us try it," said Marco.

This plan was decided upon, and so, when the snow squall was entirely over and the sun had come out Marco and Forester, taking their departure from the great tree and guiding their course by the sun, the travelers set out, proceeding as nearly in a straight line as possible, intending to go on in that manner until they should come to some stream, and then to follow the stream down to the river. The plan succeeded perfectly well. They soon descended into a valley, where they found a little brook flowing over a bed of moss-covered stones. They followed this brook down for about a mile, when they came to a junction between the brook that they were following and another one. After this junction of course the stream was larger, and in many places they found it difficult to get along. The way was encumbered with bushes, rocks, and fallen trees, and in one place the stream flowed in a foaming torrent through the bottom of a deep chasm, with sides rising directly out of the water. Here the travelers were obliged to find a way at a distance from the brook--guiding themselves, however, by the sound of its roaring. After passing the chasm, they got back to the stream again.

They came out into the open country about one o'clock, and found to their great joy that they were very near the place where the horses were pastured. The horses were all ready for them, and Forester and Marco mounted them immediately, and set out on their return home.

THE RIDE.

The Ride.

It was very pleasant riding along at their ease on horseback, after all the dangers and fatigues that they had encountered. A part of the way the road which they took lay along the shore of the river. Marco enjoyed this part of the ride very much indeed.

They reached home about sunset, with an excellent appetite for supper. Marco was very enthusiastic in his manner of giving his aunt Forester an account of his adventures, and he said, in conclusion, that he would just as lief get lost in the woods as not. It was good fun.

Lightning Source UK Ltd.
Milton Keynes UK
UKHW010746271222
414464UK00004B/282